Routledge Revivals

Duties of the Senior Accountant

Duties of the Senior Accountant

F. W. Thornton

Routledge Revivals
Routledge
Taylor & Francis Group

First published in 1988 by Garland Publishing, Inc.

This edition first published in 2018 by Routledge
2 Park Square, Milton Park, Abingdon, Oxon, OX14 4RN
and by Routledge
52 Vanderbilt Avenue, New York, NY 10017, USA

Routledge is an imprint of the Taylor & Francis Group, an informa business

Publisher's Note
The publisher has gone to great lengths to ensure the quality of this reprint but points out that some imperfections in the original copies may be apparent.

Disclaimer
The publisher has made every effort to trace copyright holders and welcomes correspondence from those they have been unable to contact.

A Library of Congress record exists under ISBN:

ISBN 13: 978-1-138-39293-9 (hbk)
ISBN 13: 978-0-429-40197-8 (ebk)

FOUNDATIONS OF ACCOUNTING

Edited by
RICHARD P. BRIEF
New York University

A GARLAND SERIES

Duties of the Senior Accountant

GARLAND PUBLISHING, INC.

NEW YORK & LONDON 1988

[redacted]

For a list of Garland's publications in accounting, see the final pages of this volume.

Library of Congress Cataloging-in-Publication Data

Duties of the senior accountant.
p. cm.—(Foundations of accounting)
Reprint (1st work). Originally published: New York, N.Y. : Published for the American Institute of Accountants by the American Institute Pub. Co., c1932.
Second work reprinted from: Duties of junior and senior accountants. New York : American Institute of Accountants, 1953.
Contents: Duties of the senior accountant / F.W. Thornton—Duties of the senior accountant / John C. Martin.
ISBN 0-8240-6144-6 (alk. paper)
1. Accounting. I. Thorton, F.W. (Frank Weldon), b. 1863. Duties of the senior accountant. 1988. II. Martin, John G. Duties of the senior accountant. 1988. III. Series.
HF5635.D97 1988
657—dc19 88-25127

Design by Renata Gomes

The volumes in this series are printed on acid-free, 250-year-life paper.

Printed in the United States of America

[redacted]

Contents

DUTIES OF THE SENIOR ACCOUNTANT

DUTIES OF THE SENIOR ACCOUNTANT

BY

F. W. THORNTON

Published for
THE AMERICAN INSTITUTE OF ACCOUNTANTS

by the
AMERICAN INSTITUTE PUBLISHING CO., INC.

135 Cedar Street
New York, New York

PRINTED IN U. S. A.

EDITOR'S NOTE

Several years ago F. W. Thornton and W. B. Reynolds wrote a series of articles for *The Journal of Accountancy* under the title, "Duties of the Junior Accountant." After publication in the magazine, these articles were supplemented by other matter prepared by the same authors and the whole text was published in book form by The American Institute of Accountants, to which the copyright had been donated by the authors.

Duties of the Junior Accountant met with an instantaneous welcome and the sale far exceeded expectations of authors or publishers. It was evidently a book needed for the instruction and guidance of the younger members of accounting staffs. Many firms bought a copy of the book for each junior member of their staffs and it was also used largely as a text-book in colleges and schools.

It was not astonishing that the book was so well received, because it was practically the first serious attempt to provide a text of that kind. The sales, however, were not purely temporary. Ever since the first edition of the work appeared the number of copies sold each year has remained fairly steady in good times and bad, and today *Duties of the Junior Accountant* is in constant demand. The book has run into printing after printing and the end is not yet.

It has now been the good fortune of the American Institute Publishing Company, Inc. to induce Mr. Thornton to prepare another text on the closely related subject of the *Duties of the Senior Accountant*. There have been numberless requests for a book of this kind which can be carried about without being burdensome and at the same time can convey to the senior accountant advice upon many of the points which will arise in the course of his work in the field and in the office.

The present book is as brief as it could possibly be made. The author felt, no doubt, that in a book of this kind there was no room for unnecessary verbiage. He felt that it was his pleasure and duty to tell, in a very few words, his opinion of what should be done. Those who are familiar with Mr. Thornton's style will remember that he does not waste words. Here is a brief, clear and most interesting series of lectures on what the senior accountant in these modern days should do.

Mr. Thornton's experience has been wide and varied. He was for many years a managing accountant on the staff of one of the largest accounting firms in the world. His activities have carried him into a hundred fields of effort, and no one in this country is better qualified to take the senior accountant to one side and tell him confidentially exactly what he should do in the situations which are apt to occur.

A. P. RICHARDSON, *Editor.*

PREFACE

Usually accountants are graded, roughly, as juniors, semi-seniors, seniors, managing accountants and principals or partners. These grades are not exactly defined, and can not be, because men develop gradually from juniors to the higher classifications; they do not jump abruptly from one grade to another.

The seniors are those accountants who may conduct an examination independently except for a final review. They may have charge of work needing perhaps one, ten, or even more assistants or of a section of a larger examination conducted under the supervision of an accountant of higher rating.

During the progress of juniors toward seniority they should learn by observation much about the duties of seniors, but, unless those seniors under whom they work are considerate enough to give them instruction in senior work, they will not have opportunity to observe some of the most important things that the senior does. Hence the present attempt to supplement the knowledge that a junior may gain in the course of his routine work.

There is no lack of excellent text-books dealing with accounting theory and practice. This book is intended to smooth the way of accountants properly trained in the art of drawing from figures all that they can tell, who for the first time are called upon to take charge of work, much of the detail of which is to be done by subordinates. The book is not intended to instruct anyone in accountancy.

F. W. Thornton.

CONTENTS

CONTENTS

DUTIES OF THE
SENIOR ACCOUNTANT

· I ·

ARRANGING WORK AND STAFF

Upon being assigned to a piece of work the first duty of a senior is to make a survey of what is to be done, the objects to be attained and the procedure necessary.

If a certified balance-sheet is to be given it will not do to assume that a simple verification of assets, even on the basis set forth in the Federal Reserve bulletin, *Verification of Financial Statements,* will necessarily be sufficient. Aside from scrutiny of profits the client often has in mind some feature of his business to which special attention is wanted. Regardless of the kind of audit required the senior should ascertain from his own firm and from the client whether or not there are any points outside the preparation of the balance-sheet and profit-and-loss account to which he should give attention.

If a balance-sheet is to be prepared for the

purpose of financing by short-term bank loans, the liquidity of assets and the amount of liabilities maturing during the term of the loan are of first importance. If financing is to take the form of long-term bonds, the prospects of profits, as they may be indicated by past results, become as important as the statement of present assets and liabilities, since repayment at maturity will be made largely out of assets not presently existing but to be acquired out of future profits. And if financing is to be by sale of new stock the profits become more important than the balance-sheet, since the return of his capital to a stockholder is not contemplated. His expectation is limited to profit to be earned.

The "stockholder" referred to means the owner or the successive owners of shares of capital stock.

Audits of smaller corporations are usually for general purposes, not primarily for financing or for the certification of accounts. The work may include the preparation of balance-sheet and profit-and-loss account for the information of the client company and for exhibition to its bankers, a general review of the accounting, and comparative and statistical exhibits to give information as to departmental economies, so as to assist in directing the business in the most profitable way, with some check of the clerical accuracy of the books and of the integrity of the client's staff.

There are also special examinations directed to some single feature of the accounts—counts of securities and agreement with some authorized book or list; check of cash payments; verification of instalment accounts; analyses of single accounts; and many others, each requiring work special in kind and amount.

At the outset consideration must be given to the order in which work is to be taken up. There may be a preferred order that seems the most logical and desirable; but availability of books and records may indicate quite a different order of work. Generally the order in which the work is actually done will be a compromise between these two.

After giving consideration to these matters the senior can so arrange the work of his staff that desired special data will be gathered in the course of the routine work.

All correspondence with the client since the date of the last preceding audit should be read and understood before work is begun. If there be a permanent file containing copies of trust agreements, charter, etc., separate from the current working papers, it should be examined. Finally, the working papers of the last audit should be looked over—these may give suggestions as to the work to be done. They must not be taken as a model to be followed blindly; the last audit may have been made when conditions were not the same as now; the last senior in charge, even, may not have been perfect. The present senior is responsible for the present audit, no matter how prior audits have been conducted.

Where work is to be done in a place distant from the auditor's home office the need for observance of these rules is great, since failure to do all the work and gather all needed data may require a needless trip away from home to get the missing information.

A little modification of this procedure may

be permissible where the same senior has conducted several consecutive audits of the accounts of a company, but a close adherence to these rules will take little time and will add to the degree of safety.

If, in the opinion of the senior, work not hitherto done be needed and if such additional work may take much time, it is desirable that the home office or the managing accountant be informed before the additional work is begun. If work hitherto done seems to be unnecessary it should not be omitted unless there is a clear case for its omission. If any contemplated changes materially modify the character of the examination, they should not be made without approval of the home office or the manager.

Having arrived at a conclusion as to the nature and amount of detail work to be done the senior must make requisition for the needed staff. In deciding upon the number required, consideration must be given to the questions as to what books and records can simultaneously be spared for the auditors' use and the number of men who can use them with advantage; the working space that can be had;

and the time allowable for completing the work. When time is restricted it may be necessary to put the client's staff to inconvenience. If so, the head of the client's office must be consulted.

It seldom happens that the entire staff can be set to work with advantage at the commencement of an examination. Clients will justly resent having to pay for the time of men waiting until work can be assigned to them. For this reason the senior should make his request for staff in such a way that not all the men will be assigned to the work at once, but that they may begin only when there is a probability of work for them to do. Spreading the call for assistants in this way is likely to be helpful to the accountant's own home office; it is generally much easier to assign two or three assistants on each of three or four consecutive days than to assign nine or ten together at one time.

From the home office the senior may obtain a list of the assistants he is to have. If he knows them and knows their respective capabilities he will assign them to the branches of the work for which he thinks they are best adapted. A man physically slow should not be assigned to counting large quantities of securities or to work involving the rapid handling of vouchers; such a man might be extremely efficient in analyzing accounts.

If the senior does not know the capabilities of his men he should obtain all possible information on the subject from the home office. Later in this book will be shown the source from which the home office draws its information; at present it is desired merely to emphasize the value to the senior of the information to be got from the home office records.

Although not in order of time it seems desirable now to say that as the work approaches completion, assistants may be released to the home office a few at a time, in the same manner as that in which they were put on the work; and the senior should never fail to advise the home office, as far in advance as possible, of the dates of the coming release of assistants from the work.

If the work be out of town and the home office be advised sufficiently in advance of the release of members of the staff it will be possible for the released men to be sent directly to another out-of-town engagement without the delay and expense of return to the home office.

When assistants are assigned to work that is to result in schedules for the working papers, instructions as to the form and contents of the schedules should be given. If left to arrange schedules in accordance with their own ideas assistants are likely to leave out some things that are wanted and to put down things that are valueless, whereupon seniors' time is wasted in revision of schedules.

Although assistants may have been assigned to take subordinate charge of sections of an examination, the manner in which they are to work is to be prescribed by the senior. Thus, if vouchers are to be checked, the senior must decide whether it may best be done by one man working alone or by two men, one calling and one checking. The method of handling vouchers will be determined by the senior, and will depend partly upon the manner in which they are filed. For example, if sufficient reference to the voucher numbers be found in the general ledger it may be practicable to vouch capital additions directly to the general ledger, or, better still, to the auditor's schedules made up from the general ledger. In other circumstances it may be necessary to vouch to a voucher register. The senior decides.

· II ·

BEGINNING AN EXAMINATION

Absolutely complete detailed audits are now almost unknown; except in the cases of very small organizations, where no adequate system of internal check is practicable, charitable institutions and clubs, even so-called detailed audits are usually examinations in which detailed work is "sampled"—a definite proportion of the items being checked. The senior fixes that proportion, and he fixes, too, the particular sections selected to be checked and the manner of checking.

At this time the senior must arrange for a systematic record of work done by the assistants. Such a record in the last preceding working papers will be worth examination; the record now to be made should assist the senior who may have to make the next future examination. However, precedent is not binding and is useful only as a suggestion. Often these records remind a senior of work that is desirable but might have been overlooked; they may omit something that ought to be done. Each sheet of the audit working papers may well show who made it up, who checked it, the date prepared, the origin of the figures.

Having assigned the assistants and prescribed the methods of work, the senior is not yet at liberty to leave the staff and take up his own personal share of the accounts. In every case, without exception, he should actually do some of the detail work in each section, working always with the assistants who will be engaged on that section. In this way he must set the pace—not so much the speed at which the work is to be done—although that is not without importance—but he must show how much scrutiny is to be given to documents, how much detail is necessary in calling postings, what vouchers are acceptable.

A company constructing buildings with its own labor may carry steel, brick, cement, lumber and other building material in stores, transferring by journal entry to the asset accounts when the material is used. Labor used in construction may be transferred from payroll account by journal entry, some reference to the payroll appearing on the voucher. Fixed assets may be carried in suspense or stores account until they enter into actual service, the transfer to fixed asset account being by journal entry.

In all these cases the journal vouchers prepared in the office of the client are not of themselves sufficient as a verification of the asset. If the vouchers be properly executed and bear all the details that the auditor needs for his schedules, junior assistants are apt to accept them without further inquiry. The senior in charge should prescribe how far, in view of all the circumstances, the entries are to be followed up. A well kept stores ledger, properly test-checked, is usually the best help to a satisfactory verification.

Payrolls for construction should be examined. They always show separately the time for each construction gang and the particular piece of construction on which the gang is working.

Before commencing a recurring examination the senior should obtain particulars of the time spent on the preceding examination and the amount of the fee and expenses. As the work progresses comparisons should be made.

When a recurrent examination, for which many comparative schedules are required, is in prospect the senior may save time by having prepared in advance skeleton exhibits, showing the figures for the comparable period and leaving space for the figures of the new accounts.

If the examination be that of a company with subsidiaries, the preparation of skeleton accounts in advance has the further merit of assuring agreement in form for all subsidiary accounts, thus making consolidation easier.

Voucher cheques may be offered in support of entries of capital additions; these are not satisfactory unless accompanied by bills for the goods or, in many important instances, formal contracts for work performed. Voucher cheques might be paid without filling in the details of the goods purchased and, if so paid, would be duly honored. Upon their return it would be easy to fill them in so that they would appear to have been paid for machinery or other permanent assets, whereas they might really have been payments chargeable to expense. A senior should work with his staff on the detailed vouching until the character of the vouchers is established, after which the assistants may be instructed which they are to accept and which are to be questioned.

Other similar liabilities to error may arise in checking customers' accounts. Some customers may have a running balance and may be shown to have paid late items leaving older ones unpaid. The presumption is that the older ones may have been paid and the money diverted or that the items are disputed and not collectible. This will be obvious to a senior, but an assistant may overlook such conditions if they are not plainly indicated. Only by taking some part in the detail work of each section can the senior be reasonably sure that the assistants, however conscientious they be, are doing their work as it should be done.

Systematically inadequate vouchers and questionable entries will have a far better chance of passing without notice if they are scrutinized only by relatively inexperienced assistants.

Upon the whole, the senior will find the trouble of doing some of the routine work highly recompensed by the lively understanding of the accounts that it gives.

After the assistants have been fairly started on their work, attention may be given to the work to be done personally by the senior. This is to be interrupted at intervals so that the senior may inspect the work being done by his subordinates.

The senior should start his work by obtaining a trial balance of the general ledger either before or after closing, according to circumstances. If before closing, he should immediately prepare a six column analysis. From this a general view of the condition of affairs is obtainable.

Cost accounts should have the senior's attention at an early stage of the examination—on the character of these accounts may depend the character and amount of work to be done by the staff. This early examination should be directed to the methods of costing, to find whether the distribution of expenses and costs is proper; whether the items charged into costs include any charges that should be taken directly as expense, and whether any class of items taken into expense should really be taken into cost.

If an examination be that of an industrial or

mining company and the plant be easily accessible, it will be worth while for the senior to visit it. Such a visit, accompanied by an operating officer, gives a lively understanding of book figures, needs for depreciation provisions, character of renewals and additions, deferred maintenance, discarded plant and inventories. The visit should be made after the examination has progressed so far that the senior has a rather comprehensive idea of the assets as shown by the books.

While the senior may and should use knowledge so gained to guide him in his accounting work, he must not permit the client to lead him into the position of one who approves the accounts on the basis of his physical inspection of the assets.

Examinations of corporations whose accounting is subject to regulation by public authorities should be preceded by an examination of the prescribed forms. Insurance companies, public utilities and public banks are all under some control as to their published accounts.

· III ·

INVENTORIES

One of the difficulties in valuing inventories arises in dividing "joint" costs. There are many industries in which it is necessary to manufacture two or more products in an uncontrollable ratio because the raw material used is split up into several differing parts. One can not manufacture sulphate of soda without making hydrochloric acid; one can not slaughter cattle and produce only beefsteak. One may know the cost of the sum of the products, but the cost of each, separately, is not ascertainable.

Where joint products are manufactured it will be found that the distribution of cost between the several products is not made by a simple arithmetical process but is largely a matter of good judgment. This judgment is primarily that of the client; but if one of a set of products be so costed that it does not sell freely and accumulates in the inventory, it indicates that the joint costs are improperly divided, with a resulting overvaluation of inventory. An improper division of costs can not result in undervaluation of inventory but must lead to overvaluation, since only items overvalued are slow of sale.

If methods are found to be correct, some of the staff may be assigned to do the "sampling" of the cost entries.

Before any assistants are assigned to the checking of inventory, the attention of the senior should be given to the methods of taking and valuing it. If a proper inventory record be kept and testing samples of it indicates its integrity, some of the staff may be assigned to compare book with physical inventories, but this should not be begun before the senior has examined and approved the methods by which the record is written up.

It is a part of the duty of the senior to ascertain as far as he can whether proper provision has been made for depreciated or obsolete material.

It is quite permissible for the senior to consult with the client as to methods of taking and valuing inventory. On proper instructions he may even supervise the actual work of taking inventory, provided that he does not take responsibility for either quantities or values, except as to their agreement with the records.

As to quantities, it is common for a client to have in his warehouse goods that do not belong to him. As to values, there does not live a man who can judge correctly of the values of all kinds of merchandise. The custom-house appraisers have many specialists to value merchandise, and even they often err. The senior should remember that he is an auditor, not an appraiser, and he must not lead the client to expect from him a certificate that the inventory is correctly valued.

The client may, however, demand of the accountant that, without taking responsibility for amounts of goods or values per unit, he certify that, using quantities and prices given by the client, the extensions and footings of the inventory sheets are correct, that the quantities agree with inventory records, and that prices do not exceed cost.

The necessary checking of extensions is, of

course, performed mainly by the staff. No accountant with the experience qualifying him to act as senior needs any instruction here as to the manner of checking or test-checking the extensions.

The best protection against grossly inflated inventory is to be got by justifying the percentage of gross profit by comparison with profits of prior periods, by comparing the percentage of gross profit with the percentages of profit on a large sample of representative individual sales, by the comparison of quantities with the quantities shown in a permanent inventory record, if one be kept, and by checking prices with purchase invoices. Finally, as an extra protection, certificates as to quantities and values should be obtained from those persons who actually took the inventories and from the officer in charge of that work.

· IV ·

DETAIL WORK TO BE DONE BY SENIOR HIMSELF

Careful examination of profit-and-loss accounts should always be made by the senior himself. They are more difficult of verification than most asset accounts and are of the greatest importance. If an asset be inflated $1.00 it means, on the balance-sheet, the addition of $1.00, no more. But it implies an inflation of profits of $1.00, which may be taken as an indication of profits in the future one dollar a year greater than the truth. If 7% be taken as the rate at which to discount future earnings, this means that the value of the business, as a going concern expected to run for, say 40 years, is overstated $13.33. This is the amount by which the value of the capital stock is overestimated by an overstatement of $1.00 of earnings in one year, where that year's earnings are taken as a measure of future earnings.

It has been stated here that the primary interest of a stockholder is not in the prospect of the return of his capital, but in the profits to be gained. If $100 be invested in capital stock, with the expectation that the company will earn 7% and will go out of business and return the capital at the end of 100 years, the amount invested in prospective earnings is $99.88½, and the amount invested in respect of the return of capital is 11½ cents—that is, the present value of $100 to be received in 100 years discounted at 7% is 11½ cents. The relative importance to stockholders of the profit account is evident.

When the profit-and-loss account has been drafted, the senior should apply certain rough checks to supplement the detail work of the staff, so as to detect any large deception that may have been hidden so well as to escape the notice of the staff.

The percentage of gross—*not net*—profit should be justified as already described; the regularity of monthly sales or, in the case of "season" trades, the regularity of the seasonal variation should be examined and large differences investigated; both growth of inventory items disproportionate to the corresponding sales and the relative volume of returned goods should be studied; the treatment of values of returned goods should be ascertained.

Where selling commission is given, even though the individual payments have been vouched, the rate of commission authorized should be compared with the volume of sales subject to commission and the total paid should be approximately reconciled.

If much interest be paid the total amount should be compared with a figure obtained by computing interest at the rates paid on the average amount of interest-bearing debt, and an approximate agreement should be sought.

The schedule of accounts receivable should be made up by the staff so as to show by periods the amounts in arrear—say those three, six or twelve months old, respectively. The senior should compare the total amount with the corresponding amount at the same date in prior years; then, comparing total sales for the two years, some idea of the propriety of the present total may be obtained. If the present total be excessive and if the excess be attributed by the client to slow collections, the arrears shown on the auditor's schedule of accounts receivable will demonstrate whether that explanation is satisfactory or not.

All these tests to be made by the senior are for the purpose of discovering any systematic error or deception that may have been too well hidden for the assistants to detect it in the course of their detailed checking.

It has been judicially decided recently that if accounts receivable have been padded heavily by the insertion of a quantity of imaginary sales entered in an irregular manner, and the excess valuation has been accepted by the auditor and carried into the balance-sheet, the auditor may be chargeable with negligence, because the irregularity of the appearance of the entries should have put him on guard.

If the procedure outlined here were followed, such an inflation would be found:

1—From the excessive gross profit ratio

2—From the irregularity of monthly sales totals

3—From the excessive amount of accounts receivable.

4—From the disagreement between actual and book inventory

even though the junior staff engaged in detail checking had failed to note the irregularity of the entries.

Small errors and inflations are not to be detected in this way; the object is to make certain that the accounts are not grossly wrong. The detail work of the staff must be depended upon for detection of smaller errors.

Briefly, the statement of what a company claims to have should be met with the question: Where did the company get it? Conversely, the claim that profits have been made should be met by the question: Where are the proceeds? If the auditor can satisfy himself that the records answer these questions satisfactorily he is not likely to be seriously deceived.

The senior should not fail himself to examine the general ledger, giving attention not only to open accounts but also to any accounts that have been closed during the period. Before concluding the work he should examine all journal entries made after the date of the closing of the books but before the completion of the examination.

The minutes of the client company, articles of incorporation, and documents relating to bond and stock issues should be examined and notes should be made of provisions for sinking funds, limitations of conditions under which dividends may be paid and other matters which may affect present or future accounts. These notes will be matter for the permanent files.

If the stock of the client corporation be listed on a stock exchange the listing application, which contains a full set of accounts, should be examined and a copy retained in the permanent file.

The accountant has been warned against overvaluations; but undervaluations may be almost equally bad. The duty of a public accountant is to state things as they are. Gross undervaluation may have the effect of creating secret reserves, which constitute a resource that may be expended without the same checks as those which surround ordinary expenditures. Things may be done with them that would not be allowed if appropriations from known funds were necessary.

Undervaluation of inventories produces distortion of profit-and-loss accounts, showing too little profit in one period and perhaps too much in another, destroying the value of comparative statistics and perhaps injuring stockholders. The senior accountant should make an effort to draft his accounts in conformity with actual conditions, and at least carry to his reviewer a clear proof of any material undervaluation that he may find. Fixed assets carried at cost are not necessarily considered as undervalued although cost of reproduction may have increased. If they have been depreciated excessively, however, cost less excessive depreciation does constitute an undervaluation.

In dealing with intentional undervaluation, tact is needed when taking up the matter with the client. It may be impossible to bring him to accept the auditor's view; reference to the home office or reviewing partner or manager is then indicated.

Duties of a senior accountant may be said to include a cross-examination of the figures.

· V ·

ASSEMBLING SCHEDULES

When the staff completes any of the schedules they should be handed to the senior for review, indexed and filed in order. By the time the detail checking is finished there should be schedules covering every item shown on the trial balance after closing.

As schedules are received from members of the staff they should be reviewed without delay and the totals compared with the corresponding general ledger trial balance items, the trial balance being marked to show what items have been scheduled so as to indicate at all times what schedules remain unfinished.

Some of these schedules may appear to be needless, as in case of schedules of bonds, capital stock and some fixed assets that have not changed since last audit. They are really indispensable, as they show what is not a certainty without them: that the items do remain unchanged.

Schedules should be so assembled that all sheets which will be consolidated to represent one item in the balance-sheet shall be marked with the same letter with sub-notations—such as A-1, A-2—for the separate sheets representing the balance-sheet item carrying the distinctive letter A. Finally, a summary sheet of the several A sheets is prepared, showing how the balance-sheet figure is obtained from the sub-schedules.

Some accountants display a tendency merely to copy a client's books and then consider that they have made an audit. Such schedules cost the client money, and, if not otherwise checked, they are of no material value in the verification of accounts. Schedules should be prepared with some definite object—not to clog the files with unverified copies of clients' books.

Precise directions for the preparation of schedules to the profit-and-loss account can not be given. In this matter the senior must exercise his judgment and try to have prepared such schedules as he thinks will explain matters in which his client or his principal are apt to be interested. Schedules showing monthly sales, with comparative totals for the preceding year, will be of value; similar comparisons of expense items are often useful; schedules showing ratio of expenses to business done are always in order.

True overhead expenses, which by reason of their character can not be expected to follow closely fluctuations in amount of business done, may be compared with similar expenses in other periods, but they should also be so examined by the senior that he may judge whether their amount is reasonable or there is cause for further examination.

Profit-and-loss schedules should be made up into a package separate from the balance-sheet schedules and should be indexed.

An excellent specimen of working papers and their arrangement is contained in the book *Audit Working Papers* by J. Hugh Jackson. (American Institute Publishing Co., Inc., New York.)

When papers are assembled, the senior must look over them and attach to the sheets any certificates that have been received, such as certificates of bank balances, of securities held on deposit, notes payable, trade acceptances, merchandise in hand and in storage, inventory certificates and others. A list of certificates needed but not yet received should be attached to the working papers and kept there until the last certificate has been received and attached to its schedule. It will probably happen that the junior staff will have gone to other work before all certificates have been received, and the senior in charge will be held responsible for obtaining and filing the certificates.

If the work be an examination of a branch of a very large business, the whole being under the direction of a managing accountant, the senior in charge of the work at a branch must arrange and index his papers to correspond exactly with the papers from other branches. If this is not done it will be difficult or even impossible for the managing accountant to consolidate the results of the audits at several branches. The managing accountant prescribes the forms of schedules.

Assuming that the senior has made an examination of all the accounts of a business, he must make up the exhibits and write the report, after which both report and exhibits must be reviewed by a partner or branch manager of the accounting firm. This is done usually before any of the accounts or the report is typed in form for delivery. The working papers, properly indexed and bound together, and the drafts of report and exhibits are laid before the partner, and the senior is present to answer questions.

· VI ·

REVIEW BY PRINCIPAL

Always there will be some parts of the audit work that are weaker than others—customers may have been asked to verify their accounts and may have neglected to do so; certificates may have been withheld; cost and inventory records may have been imperfect; doubts may exist as to the reasonableness of reserves. In all such cases the senior should not attempt to "get by" with the least amount of trouble, but he should point out persistently any weak features of the examination which he may think exist.

A senior who is once detected in the act of smoothing over defects in order that the partner who reviews the work may not know of them is forever barred from complete trust and will find promotion limited.

Partners' time is valuable; the senior should try to present his work and explain his ideas about it as briefly as possible consistent with a clear exposition of the facts. At the same time, if there be any questionable matter involved in the work he must, if necessary, force it upon the attention of the reviewer. If trouble should come later because of such a matter, the excuse that the partner was too busy to listen would not be accepted.

When accounts have been made up correctly in accordance with the records, the senior's work is not completed. If the work has been done properly the senior should have formed definite opinions as to the amount of faith that may be put in the records and the system of accounting, the faults and weaknesses of methods in use and the possibilities of improvement. These conclusions should be laid concisely before the reviewing partner.

Some reviewing partners hold on their desks, unopened, the working papers, report and exhibits and, before taking up the formal review, ask questions of the senior in charge. Such questions may be: "Is the company prosperous?" "Has any branch of the business shown marked increase or decrease?" "Is that branch a profitable one?" "Are collections reasonably good?" "Who signs cheques?" "Does the president spend much time in the office?" "Is the internal check good?" "Is the current financial position as good as last year?" "Are there any weak points in the audit?"

These questions are asked partly to get an idea of the matters that need most painstaking review and partly to test the thoroughness with which the senior has grasped the situation.

In answering such questions it will be well not to refer to the working papers; the senior should be able to answer most of such general questions without help. His ability to do senior work will be measured by the readiness, correctness and intelligence with which such questions are answered without help from records.

Before submitting to a reviewer any report and accounts, it is worth while for the senior to give to report and accounts a little private review, dropping for the moment consideration of routine detail and asking himself questions such as those recited above. Not more than half an hour should be needed to do this.

When this has been done the senior should

make up a memorandum showing briefly the points needing special attention by the reviewer, noting on the list the schedules that will be required to give information on those points.

· VII ·

DIFFERING WAYS OF DRAFTING REPORTS

Some accounting firms have their reports written by the accountants who have actually supervised the examinations, and these reports are afterward reviewed and perhaps revised by a partner of the firm. Other firms have the reports written by report writers—men who do not actually make examinations but, because they write good English and are experienced in writing reports in a manner approved by their firms, are assigned to make up the reports from information supplied by the accountants who have actually had charge of work.

Faults of the first system are that reports by several seniors are apt to be of somewhat uneven quality and that more work is placed on the shoulders of the partners—which is hard on partners but good for reports. Some of its merits are that a report written by an accountant who did the work will probably be more accurate in statement, more alive, less monotonous than a report written at second-hand by a report writer. The senior benefits by practice in writing reports; his style improves; he realizes better what a report should contain, and in the course of future audits is better informed as to the data that may be useful.

The errors that creep in when a tale goes from one person to another are well known.

The second system produces smooth, even reports, very well written, rather conservative and perhaps liable to be monotonous. Things that would occur to a senior writing his own report may not be brought out; the report writer, not having first-hand knowledge, is apt to be over cautious and to omit things of real value. If the senior have, in the first place, written a full report as a suggestion to the report writer the case becomes similar to that where a partner reviews the draft of the working accountant; but there is interposed between the working accountant and the partner the mind of a writer dealing only with second-hand information.

It is best for a senior to write a complete report in all cases, whether it be submitted to a partner, to a report writer or not to anyone. Ability to write a good report is a qualification that every senior should have.

After many days, perhaps weeks, of work the client gets a report or certificate, nothing more. The report should be of sufficient value to justify the expenditure of time and money. It is not enough that conventional items should be dealt with in a conventional way; it is even worse when seniors follow closely the form and even the wording of an earlier report, changing only the figures. During the entire examination the senior should be looking out for information which may be of use to the client; when he gets such information he should see that it goes into the report.

There are a few cases, especially in examinations of insurance companies, where set forms of report are required. These are cases where the auditor is not employed primarily to give advice but only to state that certain rules have been complied with, that the cash is correct, that the clerical work is accurate and that the entries are supported by proper vouchers. Even in these audits the set forms are used only with reference to some of the items and the auditor is free to comment appropriately about other matters. Such reports are not called certificates, but they are certificates in substance, hence their conventional form.

· VIII ·

PREPARATION OF TYPED REPORT

When papers, report and exhibits have been reviewed, perhaps revised, and finally approved by the reviewing partner or manager, they are to be typed for delivery. The senior attends to that; he delivers to the stenographic department the papers to be typed, gives the clerks any explanations they may require, and advises them of the time when the report and other papers should be ready. In arranging for typing where there are voluminous exhibits, the practice, followed by some seniors, of getting together all the exhibits before any are given out to typists, then rushing them into the department, is bad for everyone concerned. Exhibits should be fed to the typing department as soon as they are ready, so as to allow as much time as possible for typing.

After typing and proof-reading, the exhibits will be returned to the senior. It is his duty to have all typed footings checked and personally to check the form of figure statements and the language of the report. After that is done, he signs one copy of each statement as being correct in all respects and returns all the copies to the department to be bound for delivery.

Then he must dictate letters transmitting copies to those who are to receive them, personally obtain the copies for mailing and present the copies and letters to the reviewing partner for signature. With the typed copies for signature there positively must be presented to the signing partner the drafts which he already has seen and reviewed.

Not until the signed copies and letters of transmittal have been delivered to the mailing department does the responsibility of the senior end. Up to that time it is his duty, not that of his staff, to see that:

Schedules are complete and support the exhibits
Necessary certificates are obtained
Papers are properly indexed and bound
Exhibits are prepared and report written
After partner's approval, papers are properly filed

Exhibits and report are delivered to the stenographic department

Exhibits are properly typed and typed figures checked

Report and accounts are bound and signed by partner

Accounts for delivery to client are mailed with letter of transmittal

This work may not be assigned to any other person, unless at the request of the reviewing partner.

After every large piece of work is finished it is the duty of a senior to report to the home office on the work of the assistants engaged on it. This emphatically does not mean fault-finding. It means that the home office should know the special abilities, traits and dispositions of each of the assistants, to the end that if any of them show capability for more responsible work they may be promoted, and that they may be assigned to work for which they are qualified.

Sometimes a senior finds a junior who is unusually good and keeps that knowledge to himself, trying to retain the junior working under him and taking all credit for the junior's work. This plan may succeed for a little while, but it will be found out in time. It is dishonest, of course.

Nothing is more valued in a senior than the habit of reporting intelligently on the ability and industry of juniors, together with a willingness to instruct juniors in senior work. There are not enough good seniors; there are too many unsatisfactory juniors.

Inclusion in a report of matter that was known to the client before audit is generally unnecessary and wasteful if the report be made for the information of the client only. A different case arises when the information, while known to the client, is not known to bankers or others for whose benefit the client wishes the information to appear in the auditor's report.

Sometimes matter that is fully known to the client should appear in the report, because it is needed to disclose existing conditions; accounts receivable, for example, may have developed a largely increased trend toward arrears. This should be mentioned in the report.

Report and accounts should contain (1) matter partly known to the client that he wishes to have assurance that the auditor has verified; (2) matter that may be fully known to the client but that he wishes to have the auditor verify for the benefit of others; (3) new matter that the auditor has uncovered that may be of interest to the client or to others who may receive a copy of the report; and (4) matter that is needed to make full disclosure of existing conditions, no matter whether the client knows of it or not.

There are examinations when no report is made but a certificate is given to accounts prepared by the client. In such cases the work of drafting accounts is reduced to a minimum, while the drafting of the certificate becomes of the greatest importance.

In preparing the certificate the senior needs all his skill. A certificate should be as brief as it can be made consistently with entire clarity and should be worded so as to cover all that properly may be covered and no more. It should not be susceptible of misinterpretation. Certificates that contain technical qualifications the scope of which is not immediately apparent are improper. It might be that obscure qualifications in a certificate would protect the auditor against legal liability and would please some clients. The senior should refuse to draft a certificate in a manner which might deceive an investor who had only ordinary business knowledge of accounts and read the certificate with ordinary business care. An accountant can not always word a certificate so that a person quite ignorant of accounts or one not giving ordinary care to its reading would be entirely safe against misinterpretation, but the risk should be reduced as much as possible.

· IX ·

PERMANENT FILES

Some accounting firms keep a "permanent file" of working papers for each important client. This is a series of records that will be needed year after year, filed separately from current working papers so as to save time in search for information. The papers so filed are records of original organization, authorization for stock and bond issues, schemes for depletion provisions, long-term contracts, sinking-fund provisions, matters in litigation and any other matters that in the opinion of the auditor should be known to auditors at all future examinations.

If, during any examination it be found that, since the last examination, securities have been issued or cancelled, changes made in the organization, subsidiaries acquired or disposed of or long-term contracts entered into, the senior should put copies of the relative schedules or documents in the permanent file.

As such papers may be needed in the far future, when the matters are not fresh in the memory, these schedules and notes should be particularly clear and fully explained. This is the more necessary, because they are not, like the ordinary working papers, accompanied by other schedules that form an explanatory context of figures.

· X ·

COLLABORATION WITH OTHER SENIORS

It may happen that part of the work of audit may have to be done in another district or even in another country in which the auditing firm has an office. This work will be done by men, assigned by that other office, who are not directly under the control of the senior in charge of the entire examination. It is the duty of the senior to advise that other office of the amount and nature of the work to be done and the date limit for its completion.

In specifying the work to be done by a distant office it is necessary to give (1) a statement of the exact work to be done and schedules to be prepared if conditions permit, and (2) a statement of the object to be attained and the use to be made of the schedules, so that, if conditions do not permit exact compliance with ideal requirements, the distant office may be sufficiently informed to make the best use of such material as may be available.

It follows that if work be done for a distant office the instructions received should correspond with those given above, and the work done should be arranged so that it can readily be used for the desired ends, even if it can not follow exactly the preferred standard set forth in the instructions. If any change be found necessary, the office for which the work is being done should be advised at the earliest possible date, not after the work has been completed. In any case the preferred standard should be followed exactly if that be possible.

Similarly it may be necessary to assign part of the staff directly under the control of the senior to work within the home district but in a locality distant from the place where most of the work is done. Assistants so assigned should be the best on the staff; their instructions should be of a nature similar to those given to an office in another district—that is, specifications to be followed exactly if possible, with an explanation of the use to be made of the work to be done, so that if conditions compel some modification the results obtained may be the best possible for the purpose in view.

Seniors having charge of audit of one out of several interlocking subsidiaries must arrange their work to correspond as exactly as possible with that of other seniors having charge of the audit of other subsidiaries. Thus, if there be an intercompany balance between two subsidiaries, and one has shipped and charged goods to a second, while the second has not yet received the goods nor taken up the purchase, or if there be any item in dispute between the two subsidiaries, it will not do for each of the seniors to make up his accounts without ascertaining the treatment of such items by the other, leaving it for the manager in charge of the consolidated audit to trace and adjust discrepancies. The two seniors must agree on the treatment of such matters and make up their accounts to conform one to the other.

If a subsidiary (No. 1) have shipped and billed to another (No. 2) goods that have not been received nor taken up by the second subsidiary a satisfactory plan is to show the accounts of No. 2 exactly as per the books and to show on the accounts of No. 1:

Intercompany balance with Sub. No. 2 per our books	xxxxx	
less inventory in transit	xxxxx	
		xxxxx
Inventory in transit		xxxxx

If there be a difference in the intercompany accounts due to a disputed item, the accounts of the subsidiary (No. 1) claiming a credit that is disputed by the other subsidiary (No. 2) should show:

Intercompany balance per our books	xxxxx	
less disputed items	xxxxx	
		xxxxx
Disputed claim against Sub. No. 2		xxxxx

and a journal entry should accompany the working papers of the company No. 1 suggesting to the managing accountant adjustment as follows:

Debit profit-and-loss (or expense, or surplus, as the circumstances may indicate)	xxxxx	
Credit intercompany account		xxxxx

the amount being that needed to bring the accounts into agreement.

In a consolidated statement it is of no consequence which subsidiary yields its claim to the other; the adjustment must be made in some way, and this is the easiest. Much correspondence and argument may be needed if an attempt be made to bring either subsidiary to the auditor's view of the matter. That is not necessary, and the actual adjustment on the books may well be left to the two subsidiaries, to be made at their convenience. At the same time an explanation should be included in the working papers so that the managing accountant in charge of the consolidation may make the adjustment in a different way if he desire. Entries on the working papers, such as those shown above, will permit any adjustment that the managing accountant may prefer while indicating the manner of adjustment that commends itself to the senior in charge of the subsidiary audit.

If the seniors auditing two subsidiaries both make the adjustments, each adapting his accounts to the accounts of the other subsidiary, the case is worse than ever. It is an effective rule to make all adjustments on the books of the company claiming credit which is not allowed by the other; but the two auditors must agree as to the manner of adjustment and must agree on the amount of the adjusted intercompany balance.

Finally it should be impressed upon the subsidiaries that a difference between them in their intercompany balance is no more excusable than a difference between two departments of a single company. Such differences are not uncommon, especially where the subsidiaries have once been independent companies having employees with some pride in the organization.

When the senior has been promoted to the grade of manager he may have a vivid experience of the exasperation and delay caused by incompatible reports from several seniors auditing several subsidiaries of a corporation. It seems a pity that seniors can not obtain that experience until they are beyond the grade of men making the incompatible reports.

The reports made by seniors in charge of audits of subsidiary branches are similar in content to reports and accounts rendered to clients, the written report being rather more informal and outspoken in character, not necessarily typed and, of course, addressed to the managing accountant in charge of the consolidated audit, and not to the client. Indeed, such reports to the managing accountant may sometimes contain opinions as to the character and efficiency of the clients' officers and other confidential matter. They are to be a frank and confidential communication to a superior in rank and dealing with all matters affecting the audit.

· XI ·

DIFFERENCES OF OPINION

If a senior in charge of a section of a large audit think some change in the figures necessary to bring about a true statement of affairs, he should not in his statements change the figures as shown by the books, but he should add to his working papers a statement of changes proposed, the reasons for changes and for each desired change the journal entry that would be needed to bring it about. Further, the draft accounts should be prepared leaving open columns for adjustments and for final adjusted figures. The manager in charge of the consolidated audit will then decide whether or not the changes should be made. Accounts made up subject to such adjustments should be arranged so as to leave plenty of room for the adjustments; balance-sheet and profit-and-loss accounts may well be written on alternate lines so as to give space for entering changes, and in the case of items known to be subject to several changes additional empty lines may be left.

Depreciation provisions are a fertile source of disagreement. Comparisons of rates with those used by similar companies are of some value but are far from conclusive. The treatment of heavy repairs must be considered; conditions affecting wear are not always the same; quality of assets when new is a factor; the extent to which the assets are strained in the effort to speed production is important; obsolescence may make a difference.

All these things should be considered and the data digested before a senior takes up with a client any proposal to change depreciation provisions.

One rough test that is of occasional value is found in tracing over a long period the growth or decrease of the book value of net fixed assets —assets at cost, less depreciation reserve—and comparing the change, whether increase or decrease, with the growth or decrease of business done. This, however, is not trustworthy where a company has started business with new fixed assets and has not yet reached the point where annual replacements may be expected to be approximately equal to the annual depreciation reserve.

In any case the net investment in machinery and plant should not for a long period increase faster than output. If it does there is ground for inquiry.

Reserves for bad debts are also a cause of trouble with clients. The senior auditor is not a credit expert, but he is not—or should not be—unable to draw obvious conclusions from ledger figures. If, say, $10,000 of accounts a year become two years old, and the client says they will eventually be collected, the senior should ascertain what amount per annum is being realized from accounts over two years old. If the sum realized each year from such accounts is less than the annual amount falling into two-year arrears the asset needs a corresponding reserve.

Of course the two-year period is merely illustrative. The age at which accounts become seriously doubtful differs with different kinds of business.

Inventory valuation is another point on which differences of opinion arise. Where clients refuse to accept suggestions from accountants that valuations be changed, the accountant can not take a rigid stand unless valuations can be shown to exceed cost or demonstrable market value. If the differences arise on questions of quality and market value the client's judgment must have precedence and the accountant must protect himself by disavowal of responsibility for prices.

If inventory prices exceed cost, except in the case of inventories of securities held by dealers in securities, the senior should not make up accounts including such valuations until the matter has been considered by his home office or accounting superior.

An exception to this rule is found in the audits for the purpose of sale or incorporation. Such sales are made on the basis of the most correct ascertainable values. When fixed assets have been subjected for a long period to depreciation and renewals or where they have been purchased when the level of prices differed from that presently existing, there is recourse to appraisal. Values so obtained may be accepted, but the accounts must clearly show that appraisal values are used.

In similar cases some current assets, especially inventories, may appear on the books at cost, although prices may have risen or fallen. Here, too, appraisal values may be used under the conditions already mentioned.

On incorporation of a business formerly conducted as a partnership it is usual to take up the assets at market—not book—values, although such values may exceed cost. If only capital stock be received by the former owners in exchange for the assets, no taxable profit accrues and the owners take up the capital stock at a value equal to that of the assets as shown by the books before incorporation.

Inventories of securities in the hands of brokers and dealers in securities usually are taken at market value. If taken at cost the difference between cost and market values should be shown on the balance-sheet. In all cases, without exception, the basis of valuation of such assets should be shown on the balance-sheet.

Whenever there is a difference of opinion

and the accountant contemplates putting in the report any unfavorable criticism of any matter whatever, the client must first be made aware of the apparent cause for criticism, and the justification of his position made by the client must be fairly recorded and presented to the reviewing partner.

· XII ·

AUDITS OF BANKS, BROKERAGE HOUSES, AND SECURITY DEALERS

An exception to the rule that the number of men employed at the beginning of an audit should be less than the full staff engaged after the audit has made a good start is to be found in audits of banks, brokerage houses and security dealers' accounts. In these audits the work begins with verifications of bonds, stocks, mortgages and other evidences of values and of cash on hand, all of which must be attended to with the maximum of speed. In theory it is to be done instantaneously; in practice, as quickly as possible.

Instead of beginning with only a part of the staff it is necessary to use the whole staff from the first, and, for the relatively short time occupied by the count of securities, etc., to borrow men from other work.

If a bank is to be examined the senior in charge should obtain the trial balance of the general ledger—whether balanced or not at the time work is begun—and from it ascertain what items there are to be verified physically. Assistants will be assigned to cover simultaneously all cashier's cages and to verify and list securities on hand. There are so many branches of this work that the senior can not take part in the actual count but must spend his time in supervision only, keeping constantly before him the trial balance, so that nothing may be missed.

After the count of cash and securities the work continues with a balancing of securities with the lists of counted securities, customers' statements, lists of collateral, etc. This involves posting the data to security balancing cards. It can not well be done by juniors inexperienced in this particular kind of audit. It is assumed that there are among the assistants at least half the number accustomed to bank and brokerage audits. If any of the assistants, regardless of their general accounting ability, are not accustomed to this work the senior must see that each one works jointly with an assistant who has the necessary experience.

During this period the senior may take a small part in the posting work, but he should give most of his time to supervision, especially to ensure that all lists of securities counted, held as collateral, owned by customers, out for transfer and "failed to receive or deliver" are duly posted.

After all security balancing cards are posted there may be some that do not balance. No card that at first does not balance should be adjusted, even if error in posting is found, except by the senior in charge. After all errors discoverable without referring to the client's books have been corrected, there may remain differences still unexplained. Data for the explanation or correction of these may be obtained from the books of the bank or brokerage house. Such corrections should all be made by the senior, whose duty it is personally to investigate any failure of the security cards to balance.

It will be found, if the audit be large enough to employ about ten assistants, that time and trouble will be saved if the senior, during the count and balancing of securities, give his entire time to making certain that all is being done that should be done, since an omission to verify at once any item that should be verified can not be rectified properly at a later date.

This is by no means a statement of all the work to be done at the beginning of a bank or brokerage audit; it is rather an indication of the way in which the senior in charge should arrange the work. For full detail of the procedure in a bank or brokerage examination, books dealing with that subject may be consulted.

As the physical verification of cash and securities should be completed at night, or on a Sunday or holiday, and before the client again begins active business, these audits demand overtime work, limited only by the capacity of assistants to continue. Whatever overtime is made the senior should always be present. It is not safe to leave the work, even for meals, unless another senior can take up the supervision, or unless all assistants suspend work for the meal.

After the work of verification of securities, etc., the audit may proceed in the same way as any other work.

Seniors are advised not to take charge of work of this kind until they have had some experience of it under the supervision of others. Of course, a competent senior, if given time enough, could make a satisfactory examination. But one is not given time; the verifications must be made without hesitation, not omitting anything, and some of the things to be done are dissimilar to anything that is needed in an examination of a commercial business.

· XIII ·

WHEN DECEPTION OR FRAUDULENT ACCOUNTS ARE MET

If a senior upon his first general examination of trial balances should find indication of intentional fraud by the client company, such as financing by sale of securities with an exorbitant amount of the proceeds given as commissions to officers or salesmen, merchandise sold on a trick chain system where customers are led to believe that if they secure more customers they will get their own purchases free, expenditures of a clearly personal nature charged as corporate expenses, inflation of values of fixed assets and issue of securities against such inflated values, or other deceptions of a similar kind, it is the duty of the senior in charge to make a hasty further examination of the doubtful matters and then to bring the matter before the client for explanation. If, after the client has stated his case, there remain doubt of the honesty of the accounts the senior should promptly consult his home office so that the audit may be dropped if the home office so instructs.

This does not mean that dishonest accounts should not be audited, but merely that there is danger in auditing such accounts if the report is to be rendered only to the dishonest client. Such a report may be as severe as the facts warrant; it may point out every wrong; it may be such that the client would not dare to publish any part of it. Nevertheless the client could publish the bare statement that the accounts had been audited by ...., an undeniable fact, but carrying some implication that the auditor approved the accounts.

In other circumstances, audit of dishonest accounts may be desirable and necessary. If the client to whom the report is to be rendered be someone outside the dishonest corporation, such as a banker contemplating a loan, or a creditor, an audit should be made and with special care to detect improper accounts. Such a company may be compelled against its will to submit to audit and may use every effort to deceive the accountant.

Similarly, if the audit be that of a branch or subsidiary company and the fraud be confined to the branch or subsidiary or to an employee of either, the audit should be made and the report sent to the parent company.

It is not desirable, even if no irregularity is suspected, to make an examination of a branch or subsidiary company unless the instructions provide that at least one copy of the report be sent directly by the auditor to the parent company.

Finally, no criticism of accounts reflecting on the good faith of the client or of any employee of the client should be made, even to the home office, until the client or the employee has had an opportunity to explain or justify the acts not approved. It is not for the senior to take the attitude of a cross-examiner. If a client defend anything that has been done the senior should note the defense, drop the discussion with the client and deal with the matter after consultation with his home office. After all, the clients may be right; sometimes they are. One should not offend them needlessly.

Fraud by an employee, unless the client is involved, should be taken up first with the client.

· XIV ·

OVERTIME AND PROMPTNESS OF COMPLETION OF WORK

Members of a staff under the supervision of a senior should not make or charge overtime without the authorization of the senior.

Overtime is objectionable. Most overtime results from failure to estimate correctly the time required for completion of work with a given staff.

Delays in the work of audit, in getting report and exhibits typed and in securing the attention of a reviewing partner occur regularly. If a senior so calculate the time of audit that if no unforeseen delay occur the accounts will be ready at a promised time, he will find either that a distressing rush of overtime will be necessary at the end or that the accounts will be late. Both of these things are probable.

If the first computation of the possible date of completion be based on expected overtime the situation is indeed bad when unexpected delays occur. There is then no chance to make up for the unforeseen obstacles.

On the other hand, by allowing for some delay from unknown sources and basing the calculation on the amount of work that can be done in scheduled hours, a senior can give assurance that work will be done at a given time with a comfortable margin of resource if more interruptions than had been expected intervene. Overtime should be a pinch hitter, not a regular member of the team.

In every case promises to complete work at a specified time should have some qualification to protect the auditor if, after every effort, he be prevented from fulfilling the promise.

As, toward the close of an examination, the senior has much work to do with schedules made up and being made up by the staff in regular working hours and as his supervision of juniors is particularly needed at that time, it becomes necessary for him to do some of his work after the staff has ceased work for the day.

On work done out of town, this is more

necessary because the account and exhibits ought to be substantially complete while the staff is still available. Matters developed in getting out the report and exhibits may indicate need for other data or further checking which can not well be done after the staff has been released.

If working out of town the senior must not leave for home until he has at least completed tentative drafts of report and exhibits.

All this implies that the senior will have to work longer hours than the other members of his staff. This is one of the less attractive conditions of his rank as senior.

· XV ·

EXPENSES OF STAFF

When working out of town the expenses of the members of the staff are paid by the accounting firm and usually are charged to the client. Allowances for such expenses are made in various ways; some firms allow a fixed per-diem amount, varying according to the cities in which the work is done, plus car and taxi fares, baggage transportation and telegrams; others have similar per-diem rates but allow some elasticity; and some follow the somewhat penurious plan of the United States government—"actual and necessary expenses". This last plan causes work for the home office and some friction.

When the first and second plans are operative the senior should see that (1) the rate is high enough to permit the staff to live in comfort and with no loss of dignity, and (2) that the staff does actually live comfortably and in a reasonably dignified way.

Expenses outside the per-diem allowance must be supervised by the senior; none should be allowed that could not be defended if the client, who in the end pays, should question their propriety. They include taxi and car fares, transportation of baggage, tips, telegrams and telephones, postage and expressage on firm papers and similar payments, but not such personal expenses as cost of laundry work. Expense accounts should be initialed by the senior before being submitted to the home office.

Padded expense accounts are not unknown. Apart from the moral wrong, those who do the padding are foolish even from the gross-money point of view. Let the small amount of dirty money gained in this way be compared with the injury to the accountant's prospects of promotion. The home firm knows. Scrupulous honesty is not a negligible qualification in a man set to scrutinize the accounts of others.

· XVI ·

INTERNAL CHECK

By "internal check" is meant the arrangement of the work of a client's employees in such a way that the entries made by one employee are directly or indirectly checked by other entries made by other employees. Some clients have their own auditing staffs.

Even though a satisfactory system of internal checking has been installed, entire reliance upon it is not safe for client or auditor. The simple fact that the system is well designed ensures only that fraud will be difficult for any single employee unaided by others.

Assuming that a good system exists, there will still be danger if those employees who are supposed to be a check one upon another be especially intimate or if the head of an office have established himself as an unreasoning dictator, his subordinates compelled to follow his orders with or without explanation. If the outside auditor ask questions of subordinate bookkeepers and find them afraid to answer reasonable enquiries, referring the auditor always to the head of the office, the internal check is untrustworthy.

Of course, the character of the employees is important. The question whether fraud could be made profitable is to be considered. Watchfulness by the heads of the business is needed.

In an office where there are securities, the temptation to misappropriate them seems to be greater than the temptation to take actual cash, and the detection of such stealing is less easy and less prompt that the detection of money shortage.

Bonds would be missed when the coupons fell due—that occurs only semi-annually. There should be a good internal check on the custodian in all cases where securities are kept, but especially so when the securities are active —when they are frequently bought and sold. Securities held for long-term investment may be deposited with a bank as trustee or put in a safe to which only officers of a company have access, but that is not possible if the securities are active or where they are held for safekeeping for others who may at any time call for them.

Internal check is also indicated where merchandise of small bulk and high value is kept and where merchandise, although not of high price, is of a kind tempting to the employees. In a factory making silk stockings, for instance, petty thefts may cause serious loss in the absence of internal check to keep account of quantities passing from one hand to another. Such internal check on merchandise is based primarily upon the permanent inventory record.

Internal check on those who handle money is of two principal kinds, check on those who have custody of money that has been recorded on the books and can be misappropriated only by false entries or open shortage and check on those who may receive money and retain it, failing to record its receipt. In the first case methods of internal check based on paper entries may be a sufficient safeguard if the check is faithfully carried out; in the second case there is little safety in anything but constant watchfulness.

It may be assumed that some employees will study the methods of check so as to circumvent them; therefore if the methods can be varied from time to time additional safety will be obtained. A senior making an audit should consider these things. Misappropriations in business organizations are not nearly as frequent as most people think—not nearly as common as in political life. When they do occur they are demoralizing. It is better to prevent them than it is to detect and punish the offenders.

There arises the question, important to the auditor, as to how far internal check can be used as an auxiliary to the auditor's own examination. It will not do to accept internal check as a substitute for audit; a certificate must not be based upon figures verified only by the client's internal check or even by the client's auditing staff, if there be one; but the amount of detailed checking may well be reduced where the internal checking system is good and the observation of the senior leads to the firm belief that the check is properly carried out. For example, if the customers' ledger be kept by a clerk who does not handle money, if monthly statements are compared with the trial balance and mailed by another clerk who also does not handle money, if the control account is in order, less detailed checking of the customers' ledger will be needed than would be proper if the ledger clerk handled collections and mailed the statements himself.

The importance of internal check becomes magnified where tabulating machines are used in the accounting; for example the income from rental of motion-picture films may be divisible between producer, distributor, star actor and scenario writer. There will be many thousands of items to be divided weekly; the tabulating machine does the work as no clerks could do it, but great bundles of tickets with little holes punched in them do not lend themselves to ready audit. Here the reliance upon the integrity of the tabulating machine work must be great. Only limited verification can be made in a reasonable time by the auditor unaided by the machine. Internal check is valuable here.

It is almost impossible to lay down definite

rules for the general acceptance or rejection of figures vouched for by internal check; it may be said, however, that, before the auditor may certify anything, the work he does must be not less than the minimum that would justify him in certifying irrespective of any internal check.

It will be clear that there is here an opportunity and duty for the senior to exercise discretion, not burdening the client with unnecessary detail checking, not certifying anything without adequate evidence. So far as internal check is designed to prevent bookkeeping errors it may be deserving of a high degree of trust; in the matter of fraud it is less trustworthy, since there may be an inducement to defeat its purpose.

· XVII ·

THE SENIOR AND THE CLIENT

To the average client the senior represents his firm; except in cases of unusual importance the dealings are between the client and the senior. Partners of the larger firms do not frequently come into direct contact with some of their clients. The senior, then, has on his hands the responsibility of representing worthily the firm for which he works.

Clients stay with an accounting firm because of their estimate of its representatives—because they like them, because they believe them to be competent and most of all because they believe them to be incorruptible. They leave accounting firms for opposite reasons.

If a client be well disposed toward an accountant, he can help greatly with the audit; his staff can and will prepare schedules, copies of agreements, carbon copies of customers' statements and other matter that otherwise would have to be copied by the accountant. Vouchers, invoices and other documents will be got ready and arranged for the auditor's use and an effort will be made to render the work rapid and pleasant.

Assistance should be reciprocal; vouchers should be kept in order; books kept clean, office rules observed, work arranged so as to give the least trouble to the client's staff. Consideration for the client may be shown in other ways. He may be kept advised of the progress of the work and consulted if any unusual profits, losses or expenses are found. If numerous small questions which need the attention of the client arise, it is undesirable to discuss each one as it appears, thereby breaking in frequently on his time. It is preferable to list them, ask the client to appoint a time for settling them and then take up all or as many as possible at one time.

When discussion of such matters does take place it should be on the most friendly plane. There is no excuse for a petty or captious attitude—it is not dignified, not professional, not just. The client should be made to feel that the auditor is his friend ready to be of service.

Besides maintaining good feeling with the client, the senior should give attention to cultivating the goodwill of the client's employees. They can be of much help to the auditor if they choose, making the examination more thorough and at the same time less costly. It is through their good offices, as much as through the goodwill of the client, that the accountant may receive copies of schedules and other documents and have his work facilitated in other ways.

Friendly employees will bring out auxiliary records, not part of the double-entry system, which assemble exactly the data needed in preparing reports. They may point out methods of easy reference. Sometimes they will suggest inquiry into matters that otherwise might be overlooked. They may give the auditor copies of accounts that they have themselves prepared.

Employees of a client should never have the impression that the accountant looks upon them with suspicion. A detective or ill-natured demeanor on the part of an accountant is foolish and tends to defeat his aims. Such an attitude is unjust to employees who presumably are as honorable as the accountant.

On the other hand, an unfriendly staff may not only refrain from extending facilities but may even throw obstacles in the accountant's way or try to lead him into error.

Trouble is saved and clients are pleased if a senior, about to decide upon the final form of report and accounts and upon adjustments of book figures, takes them up with the client, arriving if possible at an agreement with respect to them.

The accountant should not accept favors from clients even though offered innocently. Such favors may not be intended to sway the accountant and may not in effect influence him, but they have an unpleasant appearance and may, quite unjustly, subject the accountant to suspicion.

· XVIII ·

THE POSITION OF SENIORS IN AN ORGANIZATION

There are not enough good seniors; probably there never will be. There is also a scarcity of capable managing accountants and the really good senior is soon taken into the higher rank.

As accountants rise in rank, the requirements other than those of technical skill become more insistent. Agreeable personality and the art of dealing amicably with clients have an importance in direct proportion to rank.

Willingness to assist juniors beyond the mere ordinary requirements, readiness to do extra work when associate employees are sick, promptness in completing work, absence of irritability, willingness to coöperate with other seniors, all are qualifications for promotion not less important than technical knowledge.

In dealing with clients the senior must consider himself as occupying a dignified and important office. He must not allow the prominence or importance of any client to overawe him in the exercise of his profession. He represents his firm.

That seniors should insist on proper behavior of juniors in clients' offices is well enough recognized. It is less well acknowledged that part of the duty of the senior is to insist that his junior staff be provided with reasonably comfortable working conditions and be treated with proper respect. The interests of the accounting firm are not served by allowing clients or the employees of clients to treat juniors disrespectfully.

In his dealings with both his juniors and his superior officers, the senior who would advance his rating will the more easily do so if he take upon his shoulders all the burden properly to be borne by him and as much more as he can comfortably carry—at a pinch all he can carry, albeit not comfortably.

In all the better accounting organizations even reasonably good seniors are kept employed through good business and bad; it is the juniors and mediocre seniors that are employed only during the busy season. For this reason the senior is more distinctly a part of the firm organization and has the stronger obligation to support his firm's standards of work. Seniors are the hardest worked of all the men in any accounting organization. The junior does his day's work, under direction, somewhat mechanically, perhaps, and forgets it when the whistle blows. The manager and partner have worries enough, but they do not have a great amount of actual clerical calculation to do. The senior must do quite as much actual computing as any of his juniors and must also bear some of the same kind of worry that besets the manager. The responsibility is good for him if he is ever to become a managing accountant or partner.

APPENDIX

Certain duties and responsibilities are imposed by law on public accountants. These are by no means to be considered as defining the duties of accountants; they set a standard far below that which accountants have set for themselves.

The laws of most states provide for the discipline of certified public accountants guilty of fraud, deceit or gross negligence. The profession expects from its members far more than freedom from these sins.

Accountants can not be too strongly advised to adopt for themselves those rules of conduct and professional integrity that the professional organizations of accountants have adopted. It is the duty of accountants to do full justice, not to confine themselves to bare legal requirements, which are a minimum below which punishment is provided.

It is well, however, for public accountants in charge of engagements to be familiar generally with the leading court decisions affecting the profession and it is suggested, therefore, that senior accountants at least read the reported decisions in the following cases:

Ipswich Mills v. *Dillon, et al.* (157 N. E. 604) "Accountant's working papers held to be his own property."

Ultramares v. *Touche, et al.* (243 N. Y. S. 179) "Accountant held not liable to parties other than his client for losses on account of his negligence but fully liable if fraud were proved."

Supplement to the
CPA Handbook

DUTIES

of

JUNIOR AND SENIOR

ACCOUNTANTS

CONTENTS OF CPA HANDBOOK

Volume 1

Volume 2

Supplement

DUTIES OF JUNIOR AND SENIOR ACCOUNTANTS

Supplement to the

CPA
HANDBOOK

Edited by
ROBERT L. KANE, JR.

AMERICAN INSTITUTE OF ACCOUNTANTS
270 Madison Avenue New York 16, N. Y.

PREFACE

THE CPA HANDBOOK is intended as a reference book for public accountants, their staff members, and students who are interested in public accounting. The Committee on CPA Handbook felt that the inclusion of material on the duties of junior accountants and on the duties of senior accountants would add to the general usefulness of the book. In outlining it, Chapters 26 and 27 were planned to cover those areas.

However, due to the amount of material to be included, it has been decided that Chapters 26 and 27 should be published separately as a Supplement and also that it will be made available for separate distribution.

A previous book on "Duties Of The Senior Accountant" by F. W. Thornton was published in 1932. A book on "Duties Of The Junior Accountant" was first written by W. B. Reynolds and F. W. Thornton and revised in 1933 by A. B. Cipriani. Developments in the practice of public accounting and in education and training of accountants since those books were written have made certain portions of them obsolete. The present authors, therefore, have used a different approach to their subjects than that in the original volumes which dealt with those subjects.

It is hoped that this volume will be of particular interest and help to students and staff members who have not progressed to the stage of supervisor. Not only should students and beginning accountants benefit from the material presented in Duties of the Junior, but also they should find the material on the senior's work to be helpful in giving them an understanding of the purpose and end result of the work in which they are engaged. The Appendix presents a general explanation of audits and auditing procedure. Possibly most readers will benefit by studying it prior to reading the various chapters.

As is pointed out in the Preface to Volume I of the CPA Handbook, "The contents, except for that reproduced from previous Institute publications, have not been approved by the Institute or by any of its committees. Users of the Handbook should remain aware of the personal nature of the views expressed, which may or may not coincide with the views and practices of a majority of the Institute membership. To make the material more useful, in many cases a variety of procedures has been given, frequently along with the author's personal interpretation and preference."

Special recognition is due for the contribution to this Supplement, as well as to the entire Handbook, made by the consultants, by committee members, and by John L. Carey, Louis Sigaud, Agnes Moger and other members of the staff of the Institute.

ROBERT L. KANE, JR.

New York
April 1953

COMMITTEE ON CPA HANDBOOK

MAURICE H. STANS, *Chairman*

STEPHEN CHAN
MARQUIS G. EATON
ARTHUR B. FOYE
ROBERT E. WITSCHEY

Consulting Editors

Harry Barnett
M. C. Conick
Chester W. DeMond
Rodney G. Dennis
Fred J. Duncombe
George P. Ellis
Kenneth Ernest
William J. Forster
Ralph H. Galpin
John P. Goedert
Paul E. Hamman
Cyril J. Hasson
Charles B. Hellerson
Malcolm Lamont
John Leighton
Lewis Lilly
John A. Lindquist
Colin MacLennan
Melvin D. Moersh
Hugh Evans Nichols
Russell V. Puzey
John W. Queenan
Percy Rappaport
James A. Rennie
John F. Schmonsees
L. William Seidman
Prior Sinclair
Earl P. Skau
Edgar M. Stover

CONTENTS OF SUPPLEMENT

DUTIES OF THE SENIOR ACCOUNTANT

By John C. Martin

Duties of the Senior Accountant

BY JOHN C. MARTIN

CHAPTER 9

General Responsibilities

The senior accountant is one skilled in technical knowledge and qualified by experience to take charge of the field work of a medium-sized or large audit engagement.

The senior normally has educational and experience qualifications equivalent to the level of the CPA examination. In fact, many firms require that staff men possess a CPA certificate before they are advanced to senior or even to semi-senior status. Normally a senior has been promoted from a semi-senior after having served as a junior and is thereby well grounded in the methods of the firm. The senior is usually required to have a college degree, although in some cases a staff member may develop into a capable senior with less formal education if he has considerable aptitude for the work and his staff training and experience are adequate.

The senior's education should include specialized subjects as well as those usually classified as "accounting." Taxes, budget preparation and control, government accounting procedure, economics, commercial law, finance, and English are taught in accounting colleges. They should be included in the senior's education whether or not he has obtained a college degree.

The semi-senior, as the name implies, is a step between the junior and senior. He is usually assigned to take charge of a small engagement or to assist a senior who is in charge of a larger examination.

Professional Qualifications

The capable senior should have, in some degree at least, all of the following professional qualifications:

1. Full basic knowledge of accounting principles and auditing standards.
2. Technical skill in application of these principles and standards.
3. Sound judgment and common sense in the application of that judgment.
4. Several years' experience in public accounting.
5. Knowledge of modern business organization, finance, and operations, and of sound accounting practice. With this background, he approaches an engagement intelligently, is able to detect possible weaknesses of internal control or accounting procedure, and is qualified to make recommendations for improvements.
6. The quality of leadership and ability to organize and direct the work of others.

7. Ability to speak and write effectively.
8. Initiative and perseverance.
9. Alertness to recognize unusual matters.
10. Aptitude for auditing and accounting.

Personal Characteristics

The senior should possess the following essential personal characteristics:

1. Integrity and moral courage.
2. Ability to meet people intelligently and effectively.
3. Tact.
4. Courtesy.
5. Knowledge of human nature with the ability to see good qualities of persons disagreeable to him and to resist being swayed by agreeable or forceful personalities into errors of judgment.
6. Pleasant personality.
7. Self-assurance.
8. Self-discipline.
9. Good personal habits.
10. Good appearance.
11. Loyalty.

Place in Staff

The senior's place in the staff of an accounting firm will depend on the size of the firm and of the staff. In a very small firm, he may be a partner and the staff may consist entirely of juniors. In a medium-sized organization, he will likely work under the direct supervision of a partner. In a large organization, with few partners, he may work under the supervision of another staff member who is variously termed "manager," "supervisor," or "principal." Herein, we will term the immediate superior of the senior as "principal" which will designate either the partner or another staff member.

The "supervising senior" or "manager" has usually been promoted from the senior staff because of outstanding ability, skill, and judgment. He is responsible to the partners and keeps in personal touch with them and with the policies of the firm. In relation to his assignments, he acts in a capacity similar to that of a partner with respect to responsibility and authority. He may supervise several examinations being conducted by seniors concurrently, or he may take personal charge of a large engagement.

He reviews and approves working papers and reports and so relieves the partners of a portion of that work, also, he usually conducts the conferences with the client. The supervising senior would not ordinarily be found in a small firm except when the supervision required exceeds the capacity of the limited number of partners.

The Auditing Practice Forum in *The Journal of Accountancy,* September 1947,[1] states that the senior accountant is graded as follows: "size and difficulty of the engagements completed; quality of the work done; number of assistants effectively employed; frequency and extent of supervision required; time consumed and co-operation in firm matters such as adaptability to changes in personnel assignments, adherence to time budgets, and compliance with promised delivery dates for reports."

In addition to these, the senior is graded by the quality of his staff relations.

Responsibilities toward Firm

Ralph B. Mayo, in an article entitled "Problems of a Medium-Sized Public Accounting Office" published in 1946,[2] wrote: "No accounting office is any better than the quality of its personnel." The senior is the custodian of the reputation of his firm in every engagement. He can discharge this responsibility only by observing high professional standards in his work and accomplishment.

The senior should be loyal to his principals, to the accounting firm, and to its policies. He should have pride in the firm and in the knowledge that he is an essential part of the organization. He should promote its development in every way possible and inspire his associates with the same spirit of loyalty and co-operation which he possesses.

The senior should be self-reliant, with an aim to perform his duties efficiently, and with as little supervision as possible. At the same time, he should be willing to accept the advice and decisions of his superiors.

The duties of the senior in relation to the audit engagement will be outlined later. In addition, the senior can do much to avoid idle time during the lighter months of the year. At such times, he may well look ahead to coming audits and arrange for the preparation of skeleton exhibits and schedules, having the previous year's amounts inserted in comparative statements to save time in later pressure periods. Working papers and schedules can be set up, audit programs revised, and much of the preliminary work done in advance of the busy season. Unassigned time will be well spent in study of his own reports, with a view toward improvement; or those of other engagements with which he is unfamiliar, with a view toward broadening his knowledge.

The senior should be willing to devote personal time to the study of technical subjects and to keep up to date in professional matters. His education is never completed, and he should seek to broaden it in classical as well as in technical fields.

---

1 See references on pages 116-17.

Responsibilities toward Associates

The senior accountant represents the firm in his relations with his assistants while in the field and, as such, is responsible for their work and their conduct. He should become acquainted with the technical abilities of his associates, be interested in their progress and promote co-operation among them. He should be willing to assist them beyond the ordinary requirements of the engagement, helping them to learn and so to advance.

The accounting firm rates the senior in part by the effect he has on his associates. The man who brings out the best in his assistants, who works with them in harmony, is particularly valuable. Occasionally a senior is retained because of other qualities although his staff relations are known to be unpleasant, but promotions usually go to those whose staff relations, as well as technical ability, are good.

Responsibilities toward Profession

It can also be said that no profession is any better than its members. The American Institute of Accountants, through its committees and publications, is striving in conjunction with other professional organization to raise the standards of the accounting profession and of its members. The senior accountant represents his profession in his relations with the client, its employees, and the public with which he has contact. He should, therefore, keep informed on the recommendations for improvement made by the spokesmen of his profession, and conform to the high standards of accounting principles and auditing practice which have been set. He would do well to study the leaders of his profession and emulate the qualities which have made them successful.

He should maintain membership in professional societies for which he is eligible, such as the American Institute of Accountants, local chapters of state societies of certified public accountants, the American Accounting Association, the Institute of Internal Auditors, the National Association of Cost Accountants, and the Controllers' Institute of America. He may have attained membership during college days in the national accounting fraternity, Beta Alpha Psi, an organization for men and women accounting students with high scholastic achievements. The senior accountant will gain by association with members of these groups and by participation in their activities.

Responsibilities toward Clients

The accountant has many responsibilities toward his clients, most of which stem directly from his special confidential relation to them. Care should be taken that information which he has obtained relative to business activities, operations, or office procedures of a client is not divulged improperly. Although the auditor has taken the precaution to obtain the names of employees trusted by the client to answer routine questions, he should be careful not to impart to them any information which they do not already have. The affairs, operations, or procedures of one client should not be discussed with another client or with the public, no matter how unimportant the subject matter may appear to be.

The accountant is required to give the client all helpful information which he obtains during the examination and to safeguard the interests of the client in every way possible. His aim should be to perform the examination efficiently with a minimum of cost to the client.

The accounting firm may be held legally liable to the client for negligence in an audit examination if loss is sustained by the company or its stockholders by reason of deception or errors which were not uncovered and disclosed. Negligence in this case is construed as (1) failure to do what a reasonable or prudent person would do in the circumstances or (2) performing a positive act which such a person would not have done. The legal defense of a negligence suit would require proof that reasonable skill was exercised although the facts in question were not discovered. It is not a defense that the auditor was ignorant of his responsibility or not qualified for his position of trust.

The financial statements are the primary responsibility of the client since they are based upon financial data which he has recorded. However, the accounting firm, by rendering an opinion on the statements, is responsible for:

1. Adherence of the statements to generally accepted accounting principles.
2. Disclosure of any material fact which affects the statements.

The auditing staff should handle the client's records with care, return them as soon as possible and, under usual conditions, not remove them from the office. Office rules of the client should be observed, with respect to hours, smoking, dress and other matters.

Responsibilities toward Third Parties

The accountant, by his independence from management, is in a sense a representative of the public in each audit engagement. He is morally responsible to the public for conducting his examination in accordance with professional standards and making a full disclosure of his findings.

There may also be a legal liability to third parties. There have been court cases in which third parties claimed injury when gross negligence was attributed to the auditor, because of the misstatement or omission of an essential fact in financial statements on which an opinion was expressed, or when the auditor failed to uncover a major embezzlement or other deception.

The accountant is liable to investors, as third parties, under the Federal Securities Acts administered by the Securities and Exchange Commission. In this instance, the investor must show loss occasioned by a misrepresentation in the registration statement of the subject company filed with the Commission as a requisite for sale of the security on a stock exchange or outside of the state of origin. In this case, there may be a defense that due professional care has been exercised in the audit examination and in the preparation of the report. Responsibility of the accountant with respect to securities registrations is extensive, and every senior accountant should be familiar with the governing regulations.

The American Institute of Accountants, in Statement No. 23 of its committee on auditing procedure,[3] points out the moral responsibility of the accountant, even though no legal liability may attach. This statement has to do with statements associated with an accountant's name, on which an opinion cannot be expressed because of the omission of generally accepted auditing procedures. The accountant is required to state clearly the responsibility which he is willing to assume with respect to every financial statement which bears his name. Reasons for the qualification of the accountant's opinion, or the denial of an opinion, must be stated clearly in order that third parties may not rely upon the statements merely by reason of their association with his name.

Although these responsibilities rest with the accounting firm, the senior accountant has the immediate responsibility to his firm for the examination and the disclosures required.

CHAPTER 10

Responsibility for Planning

The senior accountant does not have the same duties in every examination. His responsibility will vary with the size of the engagement somewhat as follows:

1. In a small engagement, he may conduct the examination alone or with the help of one assistant.
2. In a medium-sized engagement, he may be the senior-in-charge with several assistants.
3. In a large engagement, he will have more assistants, possibly including other seniors. He may conduct the examination under the direct supervision of a principal or he may be in full charge.
4. He may supervise several small engagements being conducted concurrently by semi-seniors or juniors.

For the purpose of these comments it is assumed that the engagement is one which requires the services of several assistants and that the senior accountant is in charge of the examination except for consultation on unusual matters and for a final review by the principal.

Starting the Examination

In current practice a good portion of a large examination is conducted at intervals during the year. Often accounts receivable are confirmed and inventories are examined at other than the balance sheet date. For additional interim work which may be done, see Chapter 14 of the CPA Handbook, and two recent articles which appeared in *The Journal of Accountancy*.[4,5] For simplicity, this practice is ignored herein in favor of the assumption that the examination is made in a continuous process at the year end. The differences between this and interim work are not significant.

There are several types of audits, although the general audit, frequently referred to as a regular annual audit, is the one usually connected with the term. This consists of an examination of the financial position and a review of the operations. The "detailed audit" is seldom used because of its prohibitive cost to the client, except possibly in cases of the examination of the cash transactions of charitable organizations. Even then, the examination of receipts beyond those recorded may be impracticable, and the evidence supporting disbursements, other than cancelled checks, is usually sampled.

There are special purpose examinations in which the auditor is expected to examine only matters which are related to the designated purpose. There are examinations which are limited in respect to auditing procedures relative to accounts receivable, inventories, or other important items in which it is understood that the auditor will not be in a position to express an opinion on the financial statements. There also is a so-called "tax audit" in which the auditor is expected to make adjustments and analyses of matters needed for tax returns, but in which there is no attempt to apply auditing procedures to the accounts.

This discussion embraces only the general audit wherein the auditing procedures are sufficient in scope to permit the accounting firm to express an opinion on the statements.

The senior-in-charge is not always responsible for the initial phases of an examination. The preparation of the audit program, preliminary review of internal control and the preliminary arrangements are often made by his principal. These matters are discussed in connection with the duties of the senior accountant since frequently he aids in their preparation and in many cases he has responsibility for them.

Review of Internal Control

Chapter 16 of the CPA Handbook is devoted to a discussion of internal control. However, a brief discussion of the topic is presented here because of the senior's responsibility for the review of internal control.

The committee on auditing procedure, American Institute of Accountants, in its Statement No. 24, "Revision in Short-Form Accountant's Report or Certificate" [6] gives a brief summary of the meaning of the term "generally accepted auditing standards" to which the accountant refers in his opinion on financial statements. In the section entitled "Standards of Field Work," the following statement appears: "There is to be a proper study and evaluation of the existing internal control as a basis for reliance thereon and for the determination of the resultant extent of the tests to which auditing procedures are to be restricted."

Characteristics of Internal Control

Internal control supplements and extends the personal supervision of owners in a small business enterprise, and in a large business it must largely take the place of such supervision. It is a plan of organization and procedures adopted within a business to safeguard the assets, check the reliability of the records, and promote operational efficiency. A proper system reduces the possibility that errors or fraud will remain long undetected. Characteristics include:

1. Separation of functions — separated responsibility for: (a) initiation and authorization; (b) recording; and (c) custody. This is possible only in a large organization, properly departmentalized. In a medium-sized business it may be accomplished by segregation of duties whereby: (a) no one person will have complete charge of a business transaction; (b) no one person or department will control the accounting records relating to that department: and (c) work of one person checks that of another without duplication of work.
2. Fixed responsibilities — responsibilities are fixed by clear lines of authority.
3. Personnel control — employees are carefully selected, trained commensurate with their responsibility, adequately compensated, and bonded.

Purpose of Review

Review of internal control is not a substitute for an audit. Rather it provides:

1. A basis for judgment of the reliability and adequacy of accounting records.
2. Knowledge of the extent of protection against fraud or other irregularity.
3. Information needed in determining the weight which can be attached to the system of internal control as an aid in selecting auditing procedures and determining the extent of the tests to be made.

When Review is Made

The initial review of the system of internal control is normally made early in the field examination, either during the interim examination or as a special phase performed in an early stage of the field work. However, many of the subsequent audit procedures supplement the initial work done and aid in establishing the degree of control and the manner in which the system operates.

One of the greatest services which an accounting firm can render a client is the recommendation of changes which will strengthen its system of internal control. Recommendations are best made in writing, supplemented by conference between principal, senior, and the client.

How Review is Made

There is no rigid formula for the review of internal control. In each case, it must be fitted to the circumstances of the engagement. Initially it is accomplished by direct inquiry, supplemented by a review of the chart of accounts, organizational charts, if any, and the accounting manual, for determination of accounting procedures and the division of responsibility. In a small or medium-sized engagement where little control exists the review is less formal.

Many accounting firms have a printed internal control questionnaire for use of their staff. Occasionally the questionnaire is submitted to the client to be filled in and returned prior to the examination. Examples of questionnaires are given in Case Studies in Internal Control 1 and 2,[7,8] published by the American Institute of Accountants, as well as in two recently published books.[9,10] The danger in having a questionnaire is that it will be used mechanically and that proper judgment may not be exercised. It has the advantage of acting as a reminder list to insure inclusion of all important phases. Small accounting firms often rely entirely on a reminder list as a guide to seniors in reviewing controls.

It is necessary to observe and test the extent to which the controls are actually operated. Questionnaires usually provide space for the auditor's verification, whether by observation or test. In any case, some written record should be made indicating the tests by which the auditor is assured that the system is in operation and effective. Because of the time involved it may not be possible to observe all control features each year except those which relate to accounting records and procedures. Others can be spread over a period of several years.

Reliance on Internal Auditors

Where there is an internal audit staff and program, greater reliance can be placed on the records. A review of the internal audit program and the working papers of the internal auditor is of great importance in evaluating the effectiveness of the client's accounting records and procedures. Auditing procedures of the accounting firm may be considerably reduced as a result of such a survey. Many auditors accept some supervised participation of the internal auditors in their examination, thereby considerably reducing the time required for the audit examination.

Control in a Small Business

In a small business with few employees it is not practicable to segregate accounting functions to provide satisfactory internal control. However, even in a business where there is only one accounting employee there can be a few elementary controls, including the following:

1. Double entry bookkeeping.
2. Control accounts for accounts receivable and payable.
3. Bonding of employees.
4. Periodic vacations.
5. Daily deposits of cash intact.
6. Prenumbered checks and, if applicable, invoices.
7. Periodic physical inventories.

If the proprietor participates in the operations to any extent, he will know what the transactions and results should be, and this in itself is a control. He may also exercise a measure of control if he performs a few simple tasks such as:

1. Opening the mail, and noting the remittances received.
2. Signing checks and at the same time inspecting the invoices being paid, and stamping them with a paid stamp.
3. Inspecting cancelled checks returned by the bank and reviewing the bank reconciliation.

If there is more than one employee, the work might be so arranged that the person keeping the general ledger and accounts receivable ledger would not have access to the cash or merchandise inventory.

Reliance on Internal Control

There is no control which is not susceptible to manipulation by collusion of employees or even by cleverly laid plans of one working alone. Internal control can only reduce the possibility of such manipulations. The auditor must always be alert to detect and recognize irregularities which may conceal a fraud. Neither can internal control wholly prevent or always detect the manipulation of records by management to mislead creditors or stockholders as to the financial position or operations of the business.

Development of Audit Program

Audit programs are discussed in general and are illustrated in Chapter 14. However, in many firms, the senior who is to be in charge of the field work on an engagement is responsible for preparing the audit program. This program may then be reviewed and approved by a supervisor, manager, or partner. The following discussion is intended as a general guide for the senior.

Types of Audit Program

Formal audit programs are of two types, predetermined and progressive. Many accounting firms have a predetermined audit program in printed form in which all auditing procedures are outlined, although it is recognized that all procedures are not required in every examination. The program is the basis for the assignment of work. It is divided into sections and the pertinent section given to the assistant as work is assigned. Such a program will require considerable alteration in the small engagement where there is little if any internal control, the client's accounting staff is unskilled, and many errors are encountered.

The progressive type of audit program is an outline of the general scope, character, and limitations of the examination. Details are sketched in as dependable information is obtained and the reliability of the records is judged. This type of program gives a great deal more discretion to the senior-in-charge in developing the detailed program as the audit progresses. It has the advantage of requiring him to exercise judgment in determining what audit procedures are necessary, and the extent to which they should be applied to the particular examination. This type of program lends itself to the small engagement where conditions vary from year to year as the client's employees are changed.

The work sheet for each type of audit program should include the following essentials:

1. Adequate space for additional items.
2. Space for initials and notations of the assistant completing.
3. Space for dates and times of beginning and completing, and time consumed.

The policies of accounting firms differ in the authority given the senior to revise the predetermined audit program or to depart from procedures of a previous year on a progressive-type program. He is usually allowed to make minor revisions, but is required to confer with the principal before any major changes are made.

Informal audit programs are not uncommon in small accounting firms. The senior is familiar with the client's business and with the policies of the accounting firm, which enables him to judge the procedures which will fit the situation. He may make the examination alone and will not need a formal program, or he may have only one assistant who is instructed orally. In situations of this kind where there is no written audit program, notations are usually made in the working papers as to the amount of work completed. However, a written audit program takes little more time to prepare than these notations.

Preparatory Review

Before the audit program is prepared, the senior accountant should become familiar with the engagement by a review of the following:

1. Previous reports, trial balances, and working papers, including the audit program for the preceding year or years.
2. The legal entity of the client (its corporate structure, partnership agreement or ownership).
3. The organization of the client (principal employees and their duties), obtained from the client's organizational chart, or briefed in the working papers.
4. The books and accounting records maintained, accounting machines, perpetual inventory records, cost system, voucher system, payroll procedures, and so forth, obtained from the client's accounting manual, or compiled for the working papers prior to the field work.
5. Accounting procedures, obtained from the client's accounting manual or in connection with the review of internal control.
6. The effectiveness of internal control, as developed by inquiry or questionnaire in preliminary work.

7. Peculiarities of the industry or trade, how the business is conducted, products, markets, financial policies, and so forth as developed through preliminary conferences with the client or with the principal.
8. The type of report desired, when due, and special data which may be required in the report.
9. Permanent files of minutes, capital changes, surplus analyses, and other data.

From this background, the senior will be in a position to decide, with the help of the principal, the audit program to be developed.

Planning Tests

The audit program, outlining the planned procedures of examination, should not be considered a formula of examination. It can only be a guide and should be subject to revisions as the results of the tests disclose the need for more or less or different work than originally planned.

The objective is always to make an adequate examination and not to complete a fixed audit program. The judgment of the senior as to the legitimacy of the facts and the propriety of the accounting for them is more desirable than assuring the mechanical accuracy of the records. It is important that amounts be stated fairly, without the necessity in all circumstances of stating them precisely. The purpose of the tests is to determine the general reliability of the records as a basis for forming an opinion.

The extent of the tests is dependent on judgment of the procedures required for a fair sampling. A thorough verification of a small number of transactions is better than a perfunctory inspection of many. Materiality of the amounts involved and the relative risk of the existence of errors or other irregularities are factors. Stronger grounds are required to support an opinion on material items than on small, relatively unimportant amounts. Procedures may be reduced for items in which there is little likelihood of material error or where a possible error, if detected, would not change the opinion. The urge of some managements to overstate the profits in periods of recession and to understate them in periods of prosperity is another factor. Certain minimum tests of footings, postings, and mathematical accuracy of general ledger accounts are necessary. If these tests disclose material errors, further tests are indicated. The judgment of the senior as to the additional work required is an important part of his responsibility.

Advantages and Disadvantages of Audit Program

The advantages of a written audit program include the following:

1. It acts as a check against the possibility of omitting procedures.
2. It lends itself readily to a division of work.
3. It provides an orderly routine and thereby saves time.

4. It provides a running record of matters completed for use during the examination and for later reference.
5. It facilitates review of the working papers.
6. It acts as a guide for succeeding years.
7. It affords some evidence in the event of a dispute as to work performed.

The following disadvantages are frequently cited:

1. There is danger that the examination will be limited to the outlined procedures, whereas other procedures may be indicated in cases where internal control is weak or material errors are discovered.
2. Unnecessary work may be done in cases where internal control is strong or when errors are not material in amount or importance.

Audit Techniques

This discussion is not concerned with audit procedures; however, a statement of the audit techniques and illustrations of their application may be interesting.

Audit Technique	*Illustration*
1. Observation	Such as accounting procedures and methods
2. Tests	Of transactions, particularly those which will disclose accounting policy
3. Inspection	Of cash, securities, inventories, and documents
4. Confirmation	Of bank balances, receivables and payables
5. Inquiry	Of management and employees
6. Computations	Of prepayments, accruals
7. Sampling (on the assumption that a representative sample will indicate the quality of the whole)	Of accounting records Of account analyses
8. Investigation	Of irregularities, deviations from customary accounting procedures or internal control
9. Scrutiny	Such as the accuracy of the cut off of closed ledger accounts
10. Evaluation	Adequacy of provision for losses on receivable or depreciation
11. Post balance sheet date procedures	Obtaining and reconciling bank statements at a post balance sheet date. Testing and evaluating the effect of entries subsequent to the balance sheet date to determine their effect on the financial statements and the need for disclosures

The senior should know well the full application of these techniques and should determine at the outset how well his assistants know them and how much assistance and supervision will be required.

Small Concern

In cases where the concern under examination is small and there is little if any internal control the senior may be compelled to review the entries in considerable detail. This would include checking more footings and postings. In this circumstance many firms require that footings be tested for all ledger accounts which are not analyzed. In general, the extent of the tests and sampling should not be disclosed to the client or employees. This is particularly true in small concerns with little internal control, for employees may obtain a clue which will enable them to circumvent the auditor by a planned deception outside the scope of examination.

Arrangement of Work

The senior ordinarily is responsible for planning the details of the conduct of the engagement. He must assign the assistants to particular tasks in such a way as to avoid lost time and confusion in finishing the engagement.

Planning Staff Needs

The number of staff members required on an engagement is governed by several factors:

1. Number of records available simultaneously.
2. Extent of allotted working space.
3. Time allowed for the examination, including consideration of when it is to begin and the due date of the report, as compared to the estimated time required.
4. The ability of assistants available.
5. The need to provide diversified training for staff men.

Often it is advisable to begin with fewer assistants and obtain more later, as required. Sometimes a junior may be requisitioned for a short period to perform a specific task, as it develops. Likewise, some may be released before the conclusion of the engagement.

Time can be saved by assigning men to the work for which they are best adapted. An experienced man should be assigned to take charge of the examination of branches or subsidiaries in other locations. Much time can be lost by inexperienced assistants who are not properly supervised.

Planning Work

Working papers should be headed and skeleton exhibits and schedules should be prepared in advance of the field work. The field work should be planned with a view to keeping assistants busy throughout the period required for the engagement. If there is joint work to be done, it should be arranged in the early stages so that later, when the senior-in-charge and other assistants are busy, there will be work for the junior.

The order of work is often dependent on the convenience of the client, the availability of the records, or the expected absence of officials. The accounting executive should be consulted for this information at the earliest opportunity, particularly as to records which may be examined only during limited periods. It is embarrassing to plan work for the concluding stages of an engagement and find it is held up because the records are not available at that time.

Frequently the first thing scheduled is the count of cash and inspection of securities which are in the office. This is particularly true in the case of banks and investment brokers where immediate physical control of these assets is essential. Intercompany or branch accounts should be reconciled early. There is an advantage in doing other routine work early to determine whether additional procedures are required. Among these are a review of the cost accounts and tests of footings and postings for a short period.

After this early work, the senior is in a better position to budget the time, for he has then gained a knowledge of the condition of the client's records and of the ability of his assistants.

In a small engagement, the records are often found to be in a poor condition. If the general ledger is not in balance or subsidiary accounts are not in balance with controls, it may be expedient to withdraw until the books are ready. The expense to the client is usually considered too great to permit the auditors to help employees with mechanical errors, unless it is requested by the management, and the examination takes longer when the auditor is hindered by extensive usage of the records by employees. It also may be advisable to withdraw if numerous clerical errors are uncovered, and the client wishes his staff to make the necessary corrections. The senior is usually required to consult his office about such a decision.

Overtime work for assistants is usually limited by the policies of the firm. The senior should not schedule overtime work if contrary to policy, except in emergencies and then only with permission. Proper planning will reduce the occurrence of such emergencies.

Before the examination begins, the senior should be sure that he has the names of the officials and key employees with whom he will come in contact. He also should be fortified by knowledge of the economic status of the client and its trade or industry. He should be certain that all working papers which may be required are taken to the client's office, as well as stationery and supplies.

CHAPTER 11

Conduct of an Audit

Basically, the task of the senior-in-charge is to conduct the field examination with professional competence and in accordance with the policies of his firm. It begins with planning the audit program, and laying out and assigning work to produce the maximum of accomplishment with the minimum of time expended.

Proper supervision of the engagement is the next essential. The senior must assure himself that the procedures planned in the audit program are followed and that his assistants are alert to recognize and report irregularities. An important phase of supervision is the field training of juniors, which will be discussed later herein.

The exercise of good judgment is another essential. The judgment of the senior applied to accounting and auditing practices, and to accounting principles, spells the success of the engagement. The junior is expected to refer all matter requiring decision to the senior-in-charge. The senior makes the decision after all facts are brought out by discussion with the junior and any required investigation is made. If the decision is major, the senior may consult with his principal and so avoid wasted time in later revisions where contrary views are held by the principal. If the matter is not of far-reaching consequence, the decisions made can be reviewed with the principal at the conclusion of the engagement.

Explanations of more than minor importance will be obtained from the client by the senior-in-charge. Possibly, minor questions may be addressed to employees but explanations of accounting principles and policies should be obtained from the accounting executive and major questions or errors referred to him.

The senior is responsible for the control of the working papers during the examination to see that they do not fall into the hands of unauthorized persons and to see that they are properly filed and indexed for ready reference.

Getting Assistants Started

As soon as the staff arrives at the client's office, the senior will assign assistants to various phases of the examination as planned. He will advise them of procedures to be followed and of the form and content of the working papers to be prepared. Experienced men will be assigned to tasks which will not require immediate supervision, leaving the senior time to direct the less experienced men.

He will show the junior how to approach his assignment, possibly working with him until the pattern of examination is developed and the character of the data is established. He then is in a better position to instruct the assistant on what irregularities may be expected, the data which are acceptable, and what should be questioned.

If there is a predetermined audit program, the senior will give each assistant the section applicable to his assignment. If there is internal control connected with the work assigned to the assistant, the senior will give him the indicated section of the internal control outline or questionnaire with instructions to observe whether or not the indicated control is being exercised.

Throughout the examination, the senior should satisfy himself by observation that his instructions are being followed and that the work is being done properly.

Survey of Trial Balance

The senior accountant usually begins his own part of the examination with the trial balance. If it is prepared by the client or an assistant, the senior will devote some time to reviewing the trial balance. He will check it back to the ledger accounts, scanning the accounts to observe the sources of entries and to detect unusual entries.

There are many advantages to the senior in this early survey, including the following:

1. He will become familiar with the accounts and how they are operated.
2. He will obtain an over-all picture of the accounting system and the operation of the business.
3. He will select any accounts which need special attention.
4. He will note the nature of closed accounts which also may require attention.
5. He will observe large or significant fluctuations.
6. By comparing opening balances with the previous report, he will observe whether adjustments made in the preceding examination have been recorded.
7. He will acquire information early which may influence a revision in the audit program.
8. By analysis of comparative figures, ratios, the relationship of inventories to cost of sales, et cetera, he may raise questions early in the examination which will require discussions with the client.

Checking and Reviewing

As completed working paper schedules are received from his assistants, they should be reviewed promptly by the senior. He should determine whether they are prepared in a workman-like manner, in conformity with the methods of the firm, and whether they disclose an adequate examination. Are they properly headed and signed by the assistant? Is there one sheet to each class of information or topic? Is the source of information noted, and the oral information obtained included? What differences are noted and are the reasons given? Are corrections indicated? Is the total in agreement with the trial balance? Does the content of the account indicate consistency? Are there errors in accounting principle involved which may have been overlooked by the junior? Have the procedures indicated in the audit program been followed?

The second step in reviewing work in progress is investigation by the senior. The best approach is to discuss the schedule with the junior, asking questions concerning the work done and his findings. If the junior is unable to answer all questions it is possible that his work does not meet with requirements and further examination is indicated. Special attention should be given to questions and explanatory comments found on the work sheet to determine what further action may be required. If irregularities are indicated they should be thoroughly investigated to see if they actually exist and, if so, whether they are clerical errors or whether there is an implication of deception or fraud.

The last step in review is to dispose of the questions which have been raised. If investigation indicates that adjustments are required, the adjusting entries should be made and posted to the trial balance working sheets. The policy of the firm may require that a major adjustment will first be taken up with the principal for approval. Either the senior or his principal should discuss the adjustments with the accounting executive of the client, explaning the errors or principles which are involved. The books can be adjusted only with the approval of the client, since financial reports are primarily the representations of the company and not of the auditor. If required adjustments cannot be made because of the client's objection, the senior should evaluate their effect on the financial statements. It may be necessary to identify or classify the account in the statements so that the facts are clearly indicated. In the event of a serious misstatement, disclosure should be made in the report indicating the effect on the statements. A qualified opinion on the financial statements may possibly be required, or the effect may be so serious as to render any opinion worthless.

Details Usually Done by the Senior

The details which should be done by the senior-in-charge are those which require special judgment and technical knowledge. In most cases, they will include the following:

1. Examination of the corporate structure — the Articles of Incorporation and amendments, by-laws, and minutes of stockholders' and directors' meetings.

2. Examination of capital stock and retained earnings accounts.
3. Examination of contracts, leases, bond indentures, and other documents.
4. Evaluation of the collectibility of accounts receivable, the sufficiency of the provision for loss, the propriety of charge-offs, and the control exercised over accounts which have been written off; also following up exceptions in important verification letters for both notes and accounts receivable.
5. Examination of the basis of valuation of the inventories, the method of handling and valuing returned sales, possibilities of obsolescence, the reasonableness of quantities, and similar factors.
6. Determination of the propriety of the additions to the plant and equipment accounts, the basis of valuation, and the consistency and propriety of the provision for depreciation. (The senior should visit the plant with an operating officer at some time during the examination; he will thereby acquire information on policies of renewals, additions, and disposals, and perhaps gain knowledge as to the adequacy of depreciation policies.)
7. Analysis and evaluation of the restrictions in the bond indentures or credit contracts, such as restrictions on working capital, dividend declarations or officers' salaries and review of accounts for the premium or discount on the bond issues, and for sinking funds.
8. Determination of what contingent liabilities may exist, by review of the minutes, discussions with the client, and correspondence with legal counsel; investigation of the arrangements with financial companies with respect to discounted notes or accounts and obtaining confirmations from them.
9. Investigation of bonus arrangements, if any, to see whether they are properly administered and whether the related liabilities are recorded. The minutes usually provide evidence of the general plan.
10. Scrutiny of the journal entries made by the client to determine the sufficiency of the supporting evidence and the propriety of the entries.
11. Survey of the insurance coverage in relation to the asset values.
12. If Federal income tax returns are to be prepared by the accounting firm, preparation or supervision of the preparation of the returns. If returns are not to be prepared, the basis and computation of amounts accrued for income taxes must be examined.
13. Preparation or review of all important reconciliations.

In all engagements, the senior will do the accounting work on the examination, as distinguished from auditing. He will be especially alert to discover errors of principle.

In a small or medium-sized examination, the senior-in-charge will do a fair amount of actual auditing in addition to the tasks outlined. In a large examination, many of these tasks will be delegated to another senior who assists in the examination, and the senior-in-charge will devote his time wholly to supervision.

Action Where Fraud is Discovered

The usual audit cannot be relied upon to uncover minor defalcations, and such is not its purpose. The accountant relies primarily upon effective internal control for the prevention and detection of misappropriations or irregularities. Defalcations are not encountered frequently, but enough cases come to light each year to warn the accountant to be alert for their existence.

Fraud is commonly defined as a false representation of fact, made with the intent to deceive another, so that he will act upon it to his legal injury. As applied to accounting, it has two phases:

1. Falsification of records to cover misappropriation of money or other property.
2. Falsification of records for the purpose of misstating the financial position or operations.

If fraud exists in the accounting records in such form as to be disclosed during the course of an audit, it will first appear as some kind of irregularity. Consequently it is the duty of the senior accountant to investigate all abnormalities. Upon examination, the irregularities may be determined to be unintentional errors, resulting from carelessness or inadequate knowledge of accounting principles or of their application. If so, there is no fraud present, because the primary requisite for fraud is the intent of the perpetrator. As an error, the irregularity can be corrected by the senior as a part of routine audit adjustments.

However, if the investigation indicates the likelihood of fraud the senior should report the matter to his principal at once. There is no universal practice in the handling of suspected fraud. Some firms instruct the senior to pursue the investigation until a conclusion is reached, after which the client is informed, usually by the principal. Other firms report the matter to the management immediately with the statement that irregularities were discovered which may possibly point to a defalcation and that a further investigation is indicated. It seems desirable that the client be notified just as soon as it can be determined that there is a reasonable basis for suspecting the existence of fraud. Since judgment becomes so important in deciding whether there is or is not a reasonable basis for suspecting fraud, the senior and his principal should ordinarily both have an opportunity to study the conditions which give rise to the suspicion of possible fraud. Frequently there may be some question as to which individual in the client's organization should be notified, and this too requires the exercise of judgment. Regardless of the evidence uncovered no charges should be made against an employee, but the facts should be stated to the client. The client may authorize the auditor to extend his auditing procedures or he may conduct his own investigation under the direction of the auditor. In any case, it is advisable to have the client obtain any desired explanations from the employee at this point.

Relatively few cases of the second type of fraud, involving manipulations of accounts by management to misstate financial matters, are encountered. In smaller businesses, with an uninformed accounting staff, many errors of accounting principle are found, some of which grossly misstate the financial statements. There is no fraud when there is no intent to deceive. Management is usually willing to accept the recommended corrections after the principles are explained.

Ordinary audit procedures cannot be expected to uncover carefully planned deceptions such as forgery of the records or widespread collusion. However, if the senior accountant suspects this type of fraud, he should report his suspicions to his principal at once. The principal may decide that audit procedures should be extended until the suspicion is removed or confirmed. Even in cases where fraud is fairly evident the principal will not approach the client or client's officer with an accusation but will tactfully obtain explanations and encourage him to state his position. It may be found that an apparently unusual situation has a satisfactory explanation.

If fraudulent intent by the client is established, the principal may find it expedient to withdraw from the engagement. The extended procedures which would be required to express an opinion on the statements after such a situation is uncovered would be costly to the client, and the moral risk would be great to the accountant.

Assembling Working Papers

After working papers are received and examined by the senior, he will index and file them according to the methods usual in his firm. Supporting papers, such as bank confirmations, are attached to the corresponding schedules.

Many firms use the trial balance as the index. The account analyses and schedules are numbered in accordance with the client's account numbers and are filed in numerical order, corresponding to the order of the trial balance. A supplementary index is maintained for other papers. This is a practical method for small accounting firms.

Another index used frequently is an alphabetical classification following the sequence of items in the balance sheet. Items which combine on the balance sheet are given a connected index classification; for instance, A-1 and A-2 might be used for separate cash accounts which, combined, equal the cash amount on the balance sheet. Under this system, the working trial balance is properly inscribed with the account identification.

Large accounting offices have their own standard methods of indexing whereby any staff member can locate schedules in any set of working papers of the firm.

During the examination, the working paper schedules should be assembled in folders conforming to the classification. When the examination is completed, they should be bound in loose-leaf binders. These may be simple, with heavy cardboard backs for protection, perhaps using the backs of working paper pads for the purpose, and the papers are held together with fasteners. If sufficiently bulky, there should be separators and index tabs.

It is helpful to have a separate file folder for assembling information pertinent to the report. This folder is also used for other information useful to the client which is to be the subject matter of a supplementary letter.

Final Check and Review

As the engagement approaches conclusion, a final check should be made by the senior to see that all work has been completed satisfactorily. The audit program should be inspected to make sure that all procedures have been initialed as completed. The working paper schedules should be inspected again to see that all notations are clear, that all questions raised have been settled, that all adjustments made in the schedules are posted to the working trial balance, and that the corresponding balances are in agreement.

The adjusting entries should be inspected and traced into the working trial balance to determine that all have been included. The senior should be sure that the adjusted working trial balance is in balance. These checks, if made carefully, should reduce the possibility of clerical errors in the report.

The working papers should be reviewed also to see that they supply the foundation of the report by providing all facts and conclusions which will go into the explanatory comments, footnotes, and the financial statements themselves. The senior should make a searching analysis of the facts which have been developed. Do the working papers explain satisfactorily a wide fluctuation which may have occurred in either assets or liabilities? Is there a reasonable relationship between the sales and receivables, inventories, and sales commissions paid? Is the relationship comparable with previous years or, if not, is the reason for the variation shown in the working papers? Are the past due accounts receivable, as shown by the aging schedule, comparable with previous years and, if not, have the variances been satisfactorily explained? Do the operating accounts bear a comparable relation to volume of sales and output? Analyses of this type applied to the working papers should reduce the possibility of overlooking the essentials of the examination and will provide a basis for intelligent comments in the report.

A final check and review should be made to be sure that all information required for development of analyses and schedules in the report has been assembled. The senior now is ready to integrate the working papers into the financial statements and the report.

Accountants usually advocate the preparation of the audit report in the client's office, where additional information can be obtained without embarrassment. In examination of small businesses, where working space in the client's office is limited and there is lack of privacy, it is often found convenient to return to the office for preparation of the report. This has an advantage in the flexibility which it provides in handling staff members. Often office workers or juniors who have not had much field work can be utilized in making mathematical calculations or checking, thereby releasing experienced men for new assignments. Other assistants can be released from time to time as the report exhibits and schedules for which they are responsible are completed.

Before leaving the client's office, the senior should be sure that no loose ends remain; that all papers have been returned to the client; and that all books and files are left in good condition.

CHAPTER 12

Completing an Engagement

The audit report will ordinarily be the subject of agreements between the principal and the client and the seniors responsibility will be limited accordingly. Such agreements, or understandings, should have established general plans regarding the following:

1. General scope of examination.
2. Form of opinion.
3. General type of report.

Drafting the Report

Having completed the field audit, the senior will have accumulated in his working papers the evidence to support his compliance with the proper scope of examination and the justification for the intended opinion. He will have accumulated, by audit and inquiry, information for the specific content and presentation of the financial statements, comments and notes and is in a position to proceed with the preparation of the report.

Exhibits and Schedules

The skeleton of the major financial statements or exhibits will have been set up in advance of the examination in the general form acceptable to the client and the firm, which the senior has adapted to the circumstances. He may then assign certain of the exhibits and the supporting schedules to experienced assistants, who will work under his close supervision.

After completion, the senior should review the statements thoroughly in the following respects:

1. Trace all amounts from the trial balance into the financial statements, making sure that any combination of accounts into one figure in the statements is proper.
2. Determine that the nature of each account is indicated clearly by the title.
3. Check all cross references to see that they are in agreement.
4. Determine that the presentation clearly reflects the facts.
5. Have all mathematics rechecked.

Notes and Comments

There are two forms of audit reports, the long and the short forms. Ordinarily, the primary report is in long form and the short form report, if required, is supplementary, possibly published for stockholders or others. Small businesses are not likely to need a short form report. Some large businesses may want only that form. In the short form report, disclosures required for compliance with professional standards are made in the form of notes to the financial statements. In the long form report financial matters are discussed, import of the statements is outlined, and the required disclosures may be made in the text matter of the report. The financial statements should contain references to the explanations in the comments, specifically if necessary, but usually by a general notation that the comments are an integral part of the statements.

The senior, through his own contacts during the examination and those of his principal, has acquired knowledge of the scope of the report which the client requires. He has been accumulating information which he believes will be useful to the client. One of the greatest services which the accountant may render the small businessman is to furnish comprehensive financial data not supplied by the client's own limited accounting staff.

At the start, the senior should be sure that the report is addressed in accordance with directions from his principal, and in a style conforming to the firm's policy, and that names are correctly spelled. The most important things should be stated first to arouse immediate interest of the reader. A condensed comparison of the operations of the year with the preceding year conveys information which is usually found to be of greatest importance to management. A condensed comparison of financial position at the balance sheet date with that of the previous year end gives an over-all picture of the effect of the operations. A summary of the financial operations for the year, stated in terms of working capital, gives a picture of where the working capital came from and what was done with it. An analysis of the variations in net profit may provide the clue that management needs to interpret the results of the operations and provide a guide to the formulation of policies for the ensuing year. Pertinent ratios and percentages usually aid in interpretation of the facts.

The language of the report should be simple and concise, free from unusual words and technical terms. In practice it is found that many small businessmen are unable to recognize the underlying facts disclosed in the financial statements and analyses. In this case the comments should interpret the financial data and clearly state the inferences which may be drawn from the comparisons.

In writing the comments the senior may be guided in general by the client's reaction to the report for the previous year. However, it is sometimes better to write the current report without reference to any other, thereby achieving a fresh viewpoint. After the first draft is completed, the previous report will serve as a check to avoid omission of anything of importance and as a basis for revisions and improvements.

Many accounting firms have style manuals or report manuals to guide staff accountants in writing reports, the objective being uniformity in style and appearance. The senior should have full familiarity with such requirements and should observe them at all times.

Opinion

The opinion to be expressed in the report is that of the accounting firm and not that of the senior-in-charge. The senior's responsibility is limited to disclosures of the scope of his examination; of the reliance he believes can be placed on the client's financial records and their compliance with generally accepted accounting principles; and disclosure of all facts which have a bearing on the opinion to be expressed. It is the principal's responsibility to determine that the working papers support the conclusions of the senior and if so whether the facts permit the expression of an unqualified opinion or require a qualification or perhaps the disclaimer of an opinion. If an unqualified opinion cannot be expressed the reasons should be stated clearly. The policies of the accounting firm may permit the senior to prepare a draft of the opinion which he believes is justified. The principal then can either accept this draft or make such revisions as his judgment dictates.

Discussion with Client

Many accounting firms have found that it is a good policy to submit the rough draft of the report to the client, and in some instances this duty is delegated to the senior-in-charge. In discussing the report, the senior explains all points not understood by the client and endeavors to meet any objections which the client may have regarding presentation. As a result comments are often clarified or rearrangements made which will be mutually satisfactory without sacrificing the standard of disclosure. Sometimes it is found that certain subject matter has little value to the client and can be omitted, condensed or its position in the report changed. In this manner the interest of the client in the report is retained for the presentation of matters which are valuable to him and not lost prematurely by inclusion of subjects which are not. In any case, harmonious relations may be strengthened when the client is given an opportunity to voice an opinion on the content of the report.

The senior should not be swayed by the objection of the client to disclosures which he is required to make in the discharge of his firm's responsibility to third parties. Instead he should exercise all of his powers of persuasion to convince the client of the necessity for their inclusion in the report. If he is unable to do so, he should refer the matter to the principal.

Principles of Statement Presentation

The American Institute of Accountants has adopted rules of professional conduct in its by-laws which govern its members. Among other things "a member may be held guilty of an act discreditable to the profession" if he fails to disclose a material fact which is necessary to make financial statements not misleading; if he fails to report any material misstatement in the financial report; if he is grossly negligent in the conduct of his examination or in his report; or if he gives an opinion on statements as to which he has failed to acquire sufficient information or if his exceptions are sufficiently material to negative an opinion; or if he fails to direct attention to any material departure from generally accepted accounting principles.

Although these rules apply to members of the Institute and are imposed on the accounting firm, they should be adopted by the senior accountant as a responsibility throughout the engagement.

Basic accounting principles applicable to financial statements are too voluminous to be summarized here. The following listing is primarily for illustration of these principles with all of which the senior should be conversant:

1. Assets should not ordinarily be stated in excess of cost.
2. Assets and liabilities should not be offset, except in the case of certain United States securities held for the purpose of paying Federal income taxes.
3. The basis of inventory valuation should be disclosed in the balance sheet or in the notes.
4. The portion of assets charged to expense, such as provision for loss from uncollectible accounts, or wear and exhaustion of building and equipment should be shown as a deduction from the assets.
5. Descriptions of the maturities and other important provisions of long-term liabilities should be shown in the balance sheet or in the notes.
6. Restrictions on retained earnings, working capital or financial operations in the bond indentures or preferred stock should be disclosed.
7. Reserves for any purpose (other than to provide for known liabilities of definite or indefinite amount, which should be designated liabilities) should be created from retained earnings (earned surplus) and returned intact when no longer required. Such reserves should be presented in the equity section of the balance sheet as appropriated retained earnings.
8. Premium paid on reacquired stock should be charged to paid-in surplus in the amount per share included therein and the balance applied to reduce retained earnings.
9. The net income should be stated clearly, without inclusion of appropriations to general purpose reserves or of material extraordinary nonoperating items, which are properly carried directly to retained earnings.

10. Long-term leases and purchase-lease agreements should be disclosed.
11. Disclosure should be made of the effect on the financial statements of a difference between tax accounting and financial recording, if the effect is material.

Disclosure of Material Events Occurring up to Time of Report

Often events occurring after the balance sheet date have a bearing on the financial position of the client, the effect of which cannot be incorporated in the financial statements. If these events are extraordinary or material, they should be disclosed in the notes to the financial statements or in the comments in the audit report. Disclosures are usually made of items such as the following:

1. Reorganizations, mergers, and sale or retirement of substantial amounts of capital stock.
2. Suspension of operations by a strike, fire, or other casualty; or an uninsured loss.
3. Plant expansion commitments.
4. New long-term financing, refinancing under different terms, or the payment of long-term debt.
5. Legal action — judgments rendered or new litigation begun.
6. Purchase or sale of substantial amounts of investments; extreme market fluctuations of investments.
7. Purchase, sale, or liquidation of a subsidiary.
8. Change in accounting methods, such as adoption of a new method of pricing inventories.
9. New long term leases.
10. Contracts entered into which place restrictions on the retained income or working capital.
11. Stock or other options given, received, or exercised.
12. Pension plans adopted or modified.

The senior-in-charge should scrutinize the records and minutes for the period following the balance sheet date and up to the completion of the examination for evidence of such events, and should also seek information orally regarding them. He should make provision in the financial statements for losses, such as bankruptcy of a customer from whom substantial amounts are due, or for newly ascertained liabilities such as Federal income tax assessments or retroactive wage increases. Full disclosure should be made of all other extraordinary events for which no provision can be made. Many accounting firms have had the experience of rewriting audit reports which are ready for delivery, in order to include such disclosures.

In the case of financial statements filed with the Securities and Exchange Commission, in connection with the registration of securities, the accountant is responsible for disclosure of material events occurring after financial statements are filed and up to the effective date of the registration.

Typing Instructions

It is common practice among accounting firms to submit typing and other instructions with the report. A facing sheet with spaces for at least the following data is commonly used:

1. Date of the balance sheet.
2. Number of copies required.
3. Binding instructions.
4. By whom prepared.
5. Date of completion.
6. Approval by principal.
7. Date of approval.
8. Due date.
9. Delivery instructions.
10. When and how delivered.

The basic information is usually provided by the senior, with the approval and delivery indicated by others.

Discussion and Review by Principal

Discussion of the audit engagement between the senior accountant and his principal will follow the line of the senior's responsibility toward the engagement. If the senior is experienced, has good judgment, and his work has been found reliable he may be permitted to conduct the examination without supervision except for the final review. If the senior is less experienced or if the engagement presents exceptional problems, he may be closely supervised throughout the examination and his authority may be limited. The degree of supervision also will govern the discussions required with his principal.

Matters to be Discussed

In general it is customary for the senior to consult with a superior in the following instances:

1. When it appears desirable to modify or expand audit procedures because the tests which were planned are deemed either excessive or inadequate.
2. Upon discovery of irregularities of material amounts which may have an implication or suspicion of fraud, either by defalcations of employees or manipulations of management.
3. When differences of opinion arise with the client on material issues.

If the senior conducts the examination without supervision, he may be required to refer other problems to his principal for decision. He also may be expected to consult his principal on the proposed adjusting entries before they are made. If he is permitted to make such decisions during the examination, they will be discussed with the principal during the final review.

The senior usually keeps his principal advised of the progress of the engagement and the problems which are encountered. He should ask for conferences with his principal whenever any situation arises on which he feels the need of advice. After the completion of the examination the principal will review the working papers to see that the audit program has been followed and that the work has been done properly.

Review by Principal

The accounting firm can assume responsibility for financial statements only after a critical review of the working papers and the financial statements. The principal conducting the initial review may be the supervising senior but a partner will always be responsible for the final review.

The staff organization varies in accounting firms and with it the review procedures. It is a fundamental objective of review that the work of each person will be checked by another. If the financial statements are prepared from the working papers by an assistant and the senior checks all figures from one to the other, there will be little reason for another person to recheck them. The mathematical accuracy of the reports may be checked by a machine operator or a junior. The principal in this circumstance will confine his attention to auditing procedures, accounting principles, and the conclusions to be drawn.

There is no standard or formula of review. It is governed by the circumstances of each examination. The reliability of the senior and the complexities of the business are taken into consideration by the principal in judging the extent of review procedures necessary to enable him to approve the statements. In all cases there should be satisfactory evidence as to the following:

1. The adequacy of the audit procedures to establish the reliability of the client's accounting records and to bring to light errors of principle and practice.
2. The propriety of the adjusting entries made.
3. The soundness of the judgment displayed by the senior in decisions made.
4. The adequacy of the disclosures in the text, statements and opinion.
5. The compliance of the presentation of the financial statements with standards of the profession.
6. The clarity and sufficiency of the notes to the financial statements and the comments in the long-form report.

In some cases the reviewer inspects and initials every working paper schedule and traces the total into the working trial balance. He may read the excerpts from the minutes for pertinent information. He will usually make a critical analysis of the statements and of the facts developed. He will question the senior concerning the items and satisfy himself that due care has been exercised in the performance of the examination and in the preparation of the report.

By the thoroughness of the review, the principal effects an internal check for the accounting firm, satisfies himself that there are no material misstatements in the report, and helps to further the training of the senior.

When the senior presents the audit report and working papers to the principal for review he should have a memorandum of the points which he thinks need the attention of the principal. He should be prepared to explain his ideas, the problems which he has encountered, his solutions to them, and any uncertainties which he may have. He should be sufficiently familiar with the facts to be able to answer questions as to profits, trends, and office practices of the client without referring to the working papers.

Individuals working as senior accountants do not always have the ability to express themselves clearly, accurately and readably in writing, but such individuals will not be really well qualified senior accountants unless they can acquire this very important ability. Because of this lack of ability it may be necessary for the principal to make considerable revision in the text of the report to present the ideas more clearly or concisely. Even in cases where major revisions of reports are required later, it is desirable that the report be written by the senior rather than by one who is not connected with the examination. The senior has knowledge of the client and his business and is in possession of information which will make the report vital to both. Continuous preparation of reports will cultivate the senior's writing ability, especially if he makes it a point to understand the changes in his work that are made by the reviewer.

Report on Work of Assistants

The senior-in-charge is expected to rate assistants assigned to him, in a periodic report to his firm . The report may be given orally or in writing, sometimes in the form of answers to a questionnaire. The senior should be fair in his appraisal, making sure that his criticism is constructive and objective. The rating should cover the technical knowledge and ability of the assistant as well as his personal qualifications, such as tact, willingness to take instructions, and conduct in the client's office. Any special abilities should be stressed. The senior will render service to his firm and his assistants alike if he makes recommendations concerning further training needed by a junior to meet the requirements of the firm. The ability to correctly appraise his assistants is a valuable trait in a senior.

Adding Data to the Permanent File

Accounting firms maintain a permanent file for each client, in which is accumulated continuing data needed for reference in later years. This permanent file would normally include such items as the following:

1. Account schedules for:
   a. Property and equipment
   b. Depreciation
   c. Intangible assets – patents, copyrights, formula, leaseholds, and goodwill
   d. Amortization schedules for intangibles of limited life
   e. Permanent investments; subsidiaries
   f. Long-term liabilities
   g. Bond discount or premium amortization schedules
   h. Capital stock, paid-in capital, retained earnings, or proprietorship accounts
2. Corporate data (or corresponding data for a partnership):
   a. Articles of incorporation, amendments, correct name of the company, and incorporation date
   b. Classes and provisions of capital stock
   c. Corporate minutes
3. Bond indenture provisions, including sinking fund data, restrictions on dividends, and similar items.
4. Contracts, deeds, leases, labor contracts, pension plans and other important legal documents.
5. Tax return data, such as surplus reconciliations, depreciation on cost bases and similar data.
6. Insurance coverages.
7. Accounting manual of client, chart of accounts, data on accounting records and accounting procedures.
8. Organizational and personnel charts (where maintained).
9. Internal control outline or questionnaire for several years.
10. Audit program for several years.

The senior should give particular attention to the accounts carried in the permanent file, in view of the permanence and importance of their content. If details are assigned to an assistant, there should be close supervision.

The client is usually willing to furnish copies of legal papers, indentures, contracts, and similar records for the auditor's files. Where copies are not available the senior should make excerpts of pertinent points which relate to the client's finances. If the client has an accounting manual, or an organizational chart, the senior should secure an up-to-date copy. If not, he should secure or prepare a chart of accounts and a list of accounting records and procedures for this file.

The corporate minutes should be reviewed by the senior-in-charge, preferably early in the engagement, for information as to new and unusual matters, such as financing, commitments and litigation, and as to dividend action and disbursement authorization. They furnish the evidence of authority for important transactions and enable the auditor to judge the propriety of the entries by which they are recorded. The senior should make excerpts of the minutes which relate to these and other financial matters such as plant expansion, treasury stock transactions, bonus and pension plans, and so on. The notes should be clear, concise, and comprehensive. Important resolutions and actions of far-reaching effect should be copied verbatim in order that the intent may be clear.

Failure to have access to the corporate minutes is a matter for exception to the opinion of the auditor on the financial statements.

CHAPTER 13

Additional Responsibilities

The responsibilities of a senior accountant are not rigidly fixed. They vary with the firm for which he works because of variations in organization; they vary with the engagement to which he is assigned; and also they vary with his status in his firm. A senior may be placed in charge of some engagements, but may be working under a more experienced senior or a supervisor on other engagements.

Responsibility When in Full Charge of an Engagement

The duties and responsibilities of the senior accountant which have been described in these pages are those of a senior who is in charge of an engagement. In this capacity, he is the executive in the field and as such he is responsible to his firm for the assistants assigned to him.

This responsibility extends to the conduct of the assistants in the client's office as well as to supervision of their work. In the unusual event of the insubordination or misconduct of an assistant, the senior will send him back to the home office at the earliest moment possible, without creating a disturbance.

The senior should comply with the policies of his firm in all respects and should be watchful that they are also observed by his assistants. He should keep his office advised of the progress of the engagement and the approximate date on which assistants will be released for new assignments.

On out-of-town engagements, the senior has charge of travel arrangements, transportation, hotel, and meals. Living quarters provided should be commensurate with the dignity of the firm. Since these expenses will usually be billed to the client, the senior should avoid extravagance which may prove embarrassing to his firm. Frequently, the senior pays most of the bills himself and can keep expenses within reasonable bounds. Expense accounts of assistants should be approved by the senior before submission to the firm. In the event that expenses are on a per diem basis, the senior should see that the staff members are not required to accept living arangements which exceed the allowance and should not permit them to choose those which would be demeaning.

Responsibility When in Charge of a Phase

The senior is often assigned to a larger engagement in the capacity of a semi-senior, working under the direction of the senior-in-charge. He is given responsibility for only a phase of the audit, and in that area he acts in the same capacity as the senior in charge of the entire engagement. An assignment of this sort is good training for a new senior and is valuable to the senior-in-charge, since less supervision is required.

The senior in charge of one phase of the engagement should be fully aware of what the job calls for and where he fits into the over-all examination. His responsibilities will normally include the following:

1. Following the audit program assigned to him, or initiating suggestions for modification or expansion which he believes proper.
2. Watching for matters which should be called to the attention of the senior-in-charge, such as irregularities, errors in accounting principle or application, and so on.
3. Supervising and on-the-job training of assistants assigned to him.
4. Reviewing the working paper schedules prepared by assistants, before they are turned over to the senior-in-charge.
5. Preparing adjusting entries required.

In addition, he may be assigned important tasks which were described previously as being done only by the senior-in-charge.

Work details usually assigned to a senior or semi-senior include these:

1. Scrutinizing asset and liability accounts to see if related income or expense accounts tie in.
2. Investigating minor irregularities such as posting errors, checks unsigned or endorsements missing, and similar matters.
3. Following up exceptions in verification letters.
4. Auditing prepayments.
5. Examining notes receivable and confirming notes payable.
6. Inspecting securities and valuable documents.
7. Confirming mortgage or bond indebtedness.
8. Examining charges or credits in appropriated earnings accounts.
9. Examining retained earnings and paid-in or other capital in excess of that assigned to the capital stock.
10. Reviewing shareholders' lists, dividends, and important capital stock changes.

Training of Juniors

The senior should always bear in mind that he is responsible for the field training of the juniors assigned to him. This duty is overlooked easily in the pressure of an examination when the senior's time is taken up with seemingly more important matters. He should realize that his own position with his firm is strengthened when he contributes materially to the training of his assistants. Training will take several forms such as instruction, supervision, demonstration, encouragement, criticism, and advice.

Instructions should be given on the procedures to be taken, how to approach the work, how much to do, what to look for, and how to do it. Instructions on irregularities will cover what kind to expect, how to recognize them, and which should be reported to the senior immediately. Instructions should be given on the form and content of the working paper schedules, the notations to be made as to the source of the information, the oral information obtained and from whom it was obtained. The senior should instruct the junior in the characteristics and peculiarities of the trade or industry under examination.

Supervision will include observation that all instructions are being carried out and that work is being performed competently and without loss of time. In the case of a new junior the senior may work with him, demonstrating the procedures and methods. If there is doubt as to the junior's understanding, the senior may recheck his work to the original records until he is satisfied that nothing is being overlooked, thereby developing the judgment of the junior.

Explanations should be made regarding the purpose and value of the junior's work and where it fits into the over-all scheme. The senior should explain the decisions which are made, the reasons for them and their effects on the statements. He should encourage the junior to ask questions and discuss with him the questions raised. He should encourage any special aptitudes which the junior may have and give him an opportunity to exercise them. He should rotate the juniors in jobs to provide them with well-rounded experience.

The conscientious senior will give constructive criticism to the junior, explaining how his work can be improved, where his conduct is weak, what policies of the firm he is violating and what type of study will benefit him. The senior should always be helpful and tactful in his relations with his assistants.

Relations with Clients

Since the senior may be the person with whom the client is in contact more than any other representative of the firm, his relations with the client may be extremely important to the firm and finally to him. If he is in charge of an engagement, his work is made easier or more difficult if he obtains or fails to obtain, the respect and co-operation of the client.

Services to be Rendered

The services rendered by the independent auditor vary with the size and organization of the client's business. In all cases where the examination is sufficient in scope to permit the expression of an opinion, the financial statements are given a degree of reliability which is important to clients, large or small. The large business with a competent accounting staff may be helped by suggestions for strengthening internal control or increasing the efficiency of accounting procedures. Such a client, being further from employees and operations, also may benefit from the knowledge that an independent authority is satisfied that its transactions are properly recorded and that its financial and operating policies are being executed properly. To the small business, the auditor in addition provides some protection against fraudulent practices, acting to some degree in place of internal control which is not otherwise practicable. The accounting firm usually furnishes the small organization with an interpretation of its financial position and operations which it does not receive from its limited accounting staff.

In an examination which is limited in scope by the client, the auditor provides assurances of the authenticity and reliability of the statements within the limits of the examination. The client in this case normally has little need of the statements for credit purposes and is satisfied that accounts not examined are reasonably correct. Care should be taken that a client of this category does not place reliance on the statements beyond the point at which the auditor ceases to assume responsibility.

Conferences

Important conferences with the client are usually handled by the partner or a supervising senior. Sometimes the senior in charge participates in conferences, and less frequently he is allowed to handle them alone. He is normally expected to handle the routine contacts during an examination.

Preliminary Conferences

Before the engagement begins, the principal will make the preliminary arrangements either in informal conversations or in a formal conference. At this time, arrangements will be made as to the type of service to be rendered, date the examination will begin, date the report is required, working space available, condition of the records, and other factors. If the client wishes to cut down the cost of the audit by having some of the work done by his staff [11] such arrangements will be made at this time. Among other things, the client's staff may prepare the trial balance, schedules aging the accounts receivable, insurance schedules, copies of reconcilements, and possibly assemble vouchers supporting the additions to property and equipment. Much time can be saved on an examination if this is done.

Conferences During the Examination

At the outset of the examination, after assistants are started, the senior ordinarily seeks an interview with officers or key personnel of the company with the object of obtaining information which will guide him in the examination. He should encourage officials to talk about the business, obtaining their views on the operations, and learning their plans for the future. After the trial balance has been surveyed and information has been extracted from the corporate minutes, he will take advantage of the first opportunity to discuss the indicated questions regarding matters therein.

Later, as questions are raised during the examination concerning any irregularities, or material errors or matters which are not clear from the records, further conferences will be held. It is not good practice to carry each question to an official as it arises, but rather to accumulate such matters until an opportunity is presented. The senior should be very sure of his ground before bringing errors to the attention of the client, and be tactful in his presentation, to avoid creating antagonism. Explanations are more reliable when obtained amicably than in a tense atmosphere. If there is a difference of opinion on accounting principles, the senior should explain his position as clearly as possible; then if he does not readily convince the client he should allow the matter to drop, referring it to his principal to handle.

Any important information obtained during the examination should be disclosed to the client and nothing withheld which would be of help to him. Major irregularities or fraud discovered, weaknesses in internal control or in the accounting system which might occasion losses, or suggestions for improving the system should be written and then presented in person with explanations. Normally, this is done by the principal with the senior present, but sometimes it is handled alone by a senior who is qualified for such an assignment.

As previously indicated, the report is usually discussed with the client in preliminary draft. If the senior handles this conference, he should make sure that the findings of the examination and the adjustments made are fully understood. The position of the accounting firm should be clarified with respect to any exceptions which they are obliged to take in the opinion.

Attitudes

An important requirement in dealing with the client or his representatives is the exercise of tactfulness, saying or doing what is appropriate without giving offense. Friction should never be allowed to develop. If in the discussion of unpleasant subjects, the client becomes angry or unreasonable, the senior should courteously suggest that the matter be deferred until they both have time to think further about the matter. He may then refer the matter to his principal with a full statement of the position taken by the client.

The senior should cultivate the goodwill of the officials and employees, for the examination will proceed with greater celerity with their full co-operation. He should have enough knowledge of human nature to be able to meet each person with the attitude best suited to him. He should be friendly and respectful with all, but not intimate. He should not fraternize in any way with the employees or officials of the client. He should be sure that arbitrary demands are not made by his assistants. He should be careful that his staff does not impede the work of the office by using records when they are needed by employees or by retaining records longer than necessary. The senior and his staff, although alert to discover fraud, should never display a suspicious attitude toward either the client or his employees.

The senior should bear himself with assurance and confidence, without being overbearing. He should be willing to listen to suggestions but not to accept unjustified criticism. He should bear in mind that, as a representative of his firm, he should be respectful to others and in turn expect respect for himself and the accounting firm which he represents.

Responsibility for Professional Standards

The CPA who is practicing as an independent public accountant is held to a high standard of professional conduct. Staff members, and especially those occupying a position of responsibility such as that of a senior, must be aware of those professional standards. The profession has accepted a code of ethics for its general guidance. Every senior should be aware of the ethical standards of the profession. As to auditing engagements, the profession has equally important standards which must be observed and with which the senior must be conversant. Many firms supply each senior with a copy of publications such as the Tentative Statement of Auditing Standards, the Codification of Statements on Auditing Procedures (both of these publications are reprinted in full as Appendixes A and B of Chapter 13 of the CPA Handbook) and similar current publications. Even though they may not be supplied to individual seniors, these publications are generally available and should be in each senior's library.

Not only must the senior be aware of the standards accepted by the profession, but he must apply them in his work. To meet his responsibility he must continually keep abreast of current developments in auditing and in accounting. He must make certain that he is technically qualified to meet his responsibilities.

References

1. Brink, Victor Z., "Senior Accountant" in Auditing Practice Forum, *The Journal of Accountancy*, September 1947, page 235.

2. Mayo, Ralph B., "Problems of a Medium-Sized Public Accounting Office," *The Journal of Accountancy*, December 1946, pages 490-93.

3. Statements on Auditing Procedure: Clarification of Accountant's Report When Opinion is Omitted. Bulletin Number 23, American Institute of Accountants, December 1947.

4. BECKERS, LEONARD F., "Organizational or Procedural Changes May Help Flatten the Large Firm's Year-End Peak," *The Journal of Accountancy,* July 1950, pages 30-35.

5. RAWLINSON, CHARLES E., "An Audit Program Designed to Eliminate Year-End Peaks by Expanding Interim Examination," *The Journal of Accountancy,* February 1951, pages 272-75.

6. Statements on Auditing Procedure: Revision in Short-Form Accountant's Report or Certificate. Bulletin Number 24, American Institute of Accountants, October 1948.

7. "The Textile Company," in Case Studies in Internal Control, American Institute of Accountants.

8. "The Machine Manufacturing Company," in Case Studies in Internal Control, American Institute of Accountants.

9. HOLMES, ARTHUR W., "Auditing Principles and Procedures," Richard D. Irwin, Chicago, Ill., 1951.

10. MONTGOMERY, ROBERT H., Lenhart, Norman J., and Jennings, Alvin B., "Montgomery's Auditing," the Ronald Press Company, New York, N. Y., Seventh Edition, 1949.

11. HEARNE, DAVID C., "How to Use Client's Staff to Cut Costs of Audit of a Small Business," *The Journal of Accountancy,* September 1951, pages 307-12.

Appendix

AUDITS BY CERTIFIED PUBLIC ACCOUNTANTS

. . . . THEIR NATURE AND SIGNIFICANCE

★

AMERICAN INSTITUTE OF ACCOUNTANTS

OUTLINE OF APPENDIX

Section I. FINANCIAL STATEMENTS

Financial Statements Reflect Judgment as Well as Facts (Balance Sheet, Income Statement, Consolidated Statements); Judgment is Guided by Accounting Principles; Company Has Primary Responsibility for Financial Statements.

Section II. THE CPA's REPORT

The CPA Expresses an Opinion; The Opinion May Be Expressed in a Short-Form Report; The Opinion May be Expressed in a Long-Form Report; The CPA's Report May Be Qualified; The CPA May Disclaim An Opinion.

Section III. AUDITING PHILOSOPHY

Audits are Not Uniform; The CPA Usually Relies Upon Tests; The CPA Often Performs Part of the Audit During the Year; The CPA Is Guided by Auditing Standards (Personal Standards, Standards of Field Work, Standards of Reporting).

Section IV. AUDITING PROCEDURES

Audit Techniques; Auditing Procedures Often Employed (Cash; Notes Receivable; Accounts Receivable; Inventory; Investments; Property; Intangible Assets; Deferred Charges and Prepaid Expenses; Other Assets; Liabilities; Estimated Future Liabilities and Appropriations of Retained Income – Reserves, Capital Stock; Other Capital Items – Capital Surplus – and Retained Income – Earned Surplus, Income and Expense Accounts; Consolidated Statements).

AUDITS BY CERTIFIED PUBLIC ACCOUNTANTS

Preface

This pamphlet has been prepared by the research department of the American Institute of Accountants to fill the need expressed by credit grantors, teachers, and others concerned with the work of the certified public accountant for a brief, but reasonably complete, statement setting forth in general terms what the CPA does in order that he may express an opinion on financial statements. It discusses some of the characteristics of financial statements and explains the significance of the CPA's report. Auditing procedures frequently employed by CPAs are described in some detail, but they are not a checklist of procedures applicable in a particular audit.

Together with *Statements on Auditing Procedure, Case Studies in Auditing Procedure, Tentative Statement of Auditing Standards* and *Accounting Research Bulletins,* this pamphlet supplants the earlier pamphlet, *Examination of Financial Statements by Independent Public Accountants,* published by the American Institute of Accountants in 1936 and now out of print. It is hoped this pamphlet will help those who are not familiar with the process of auditing gain a better understanding of the Certified Public Accountant's work and his responsibilities.

CARMAN G. BLOUGH, *Director of Research*
AMERICAN INSTITUTE OF ACCOUNTANTS

May 1950

Appendix

AUDITS BY CERTIFIED PUBLIC ACCOUNTANTS

Introduction

A certified public accountant's opinion as to the fairness of financial statements is important to all who use such statements. The opinion states whether or not the certified public accountant considers the financial position of the company and the results of its operations to be presented fairly in conformity with generally accepted accounting principles applied on a consistent basis.

Despite the reliance which is placed upon the opinion of a certified public accountant, few people outside the accounting profession understand how he reaches it. Many believe there is something mysterious about the process. The principal purpose of this pamphlet is to help those who have had little or no accounting training gain a better understanding of how the certified public accountant makes an audit. It discusses the nature and characteristics of financial statements, noting particularly their limitations, and outlines the certified public accountant's responsibilities in reporting upon them. Many of the procedures frequently employed in carrying out those responsibilities are described in general terms.

Principal Uses of Pamphlet

Particular attention has been given to the need expressed by bankers and other credit grantors for a summary of the basic considerations usually involved in making audits of small and medium-sized manufacturing or mercantile companies. Accordingly, this pamphlet is concerned primarily with the certified public accountant's work in connection with *audited* financial statements submitted to bankers or other credit grantors of such companies.

This pamphlet should also be helpful to users of financial statements generally. Teachers of auditing, and those concerned with staff training in public accounting firms might advantageously employ it as an introduction to the series of *Case Studies in Auditing Procedure* which the committee on auditing procedure of the American Institute of Accountants is currently sponsoring.

While not intended as a statement of "minimum procedures" for conducting an audit or as a "standard audit program," the procedures outlined in this pamphlet are all applied in actual practice, though they will seldom, if ever, all be applied in the same engagement. Accounting practitioners, too, may therefore find the discussions suggestive of some of the procedures which might be applicable in a particular audit.

Auditing Services

The type of work discussed in this pamphlet is the *examination,* or *audit* as it is commonly called, which the certified public accountant makes as a basis for an opinion on the fairness with which financial position and results of operations are presented. That type of work consists of a searching, analytical review of the books, vouchers, and other evidence supporting the information set forth in the financial statements, and contemplates the preparation of a written report in which the certified public accountant states his findings. In the course of his audit, he employs a variety of techniques and tests, selecting the procedures which in his judgment and experience are best suited to each engagement.

Other Services

In addition to conducting audits, many certified public accountants perform professional services and report on matters related more to their capacity as expert accountants than to their capacity as auditors. For example, they may be engaged to prepare financial statements from the books with little or no audit verification. They may be engaged to make analyses of certain accounts, or to make special studies. Certified public accountants often render expert advice on such matters as accounting methods and procedures, tax accounting, reports to governmental agencies, and general business matters.

Those services are of great value to the business community and require a high degree of professional skill. In performing them the certified public accountant may employ some auditing procedures, but not usually to a sufficient extent to provide an informed opinion as to the fairness of any general financial statements that may be included in his report.

The Opinion

Depending upon the circumstances, the certified public accountant (1) expresses an unqualified opinion, (2) expresses a qualified opinion, or (3) disclaims an opinion on the statements taken as a whole. Thus, when a certified public accountant finds he cannot express an unqualified opinion, he weighs the qualifications or exceptions he considers necessary with respect to his opinion to determine their significance. If they are not such as to destroy the significance of an opinion with respect to the statements taken as a whole, he renders a properly qualified opinion. If the exceptions are so material as to negative an opinion on the statements taken as a whole, he is under obligation to disclaim such an opinion, giving his reasons why. His disclaimer of opinion is indicated either by a specific statement in his report to the effect that an opinion cannot be expressed, or, if no report accompanies financial statements with which his name is associated, by a note, such as *Prepared from the Books without Audit,* on the face of each statement. Since the degree of responsibility the certified public accountant takes for financial statements varies with the circumstances of each audit, it is important to read his report carefully.

CPA Requirements

Users of financial statements look to the certified public accountant's report in determining the credibility of financial statements because they know it presents the conclusions of an independent expert in accounting and auditing. Certified public accountants must demonstrate their high professional qualifications to state boards of accountancy before receiving their certificates, and must observe strict standards in the performance of their work. The right to use the title Certified Public Accountant, or CPA, is granted by each state and territory, and by the District of Columbia, only to persons who, with minor special exceptions, present satisfactory evidence as to their character, training, and experience, and who pass an examination to test their knowledge of the matters with which they will be called upon to deal. In many states anyone can practice as a *public* accountant. Some states require public accountants to be registered. However, in the great majority of states, only *certified* public accountants have passed a written examination given under state supervision.

Professional Societies

A number of organizations have been formed to further the development of the accounting profession; principally, the American Institute of Accountants, which is the national organization of certified public accountants, and numerous state societies, some with local chapters. These organizations are constantly engaged in the study of various phases of the certified public accountant's work. Through their efforts to maintain high ethical and professional standards, they have contributed greatly to the development of the concepts discussed in the succeeding sections of this pamphlet.

Section I: FINANCIAL STATEMENTS

Financial statements ordinarily consist of a balance sheet, an income statement, a statement of retained income (earned surplus), and footnotes. If appropriate, they are accompanied by schedules showing the details of various items on the statements.

The purpose of the balance sheet is to present a summary of the assets, liabilities, and capital of a company as of a specified date. The income statement summarizes the results of operations for a period, often the year ending on the date of the balance sheet. The statement of retained income sets forth increases or reductions during the period in the undistributed earnings of the business. Footnotes are often provided to explain items more fully than is possible in the captions. They are considered an integral part of the financial statements.

Financial Statements Reflect Judgment as well as Facts

Perhaps no class of information is so imperfectly appraised by its readers as that contained in financial statements. Many regard the statements as mathematically accurate presentations of financial facts. Others regard them with complete skepticism.

Actually, the values of most items in financial statements cannot be measured exactly. By their nature, many of the amounts shown have to be approximations and represent the best estimates which those responsible for the statement can make. The items which, in part at least, are subject to approximation are among the most important in the financial statements. Despite these limitations, however, financial statements serve their purposes well. They merit acceptance and confidence as the fairest presentation of the financial position and operating results of a business which it has been possible to devise.

The reasons approximations often have to be made may be easier to understand if some examples of items which cannot be measured exactly — items as to which judgment is an important factor — are considered.

Balance Sheet

The item, accounts receivable, is an example. The total of customers' accounts can be stated with approximate accuracy, but provision for the uncollectible element in these accounts is a matter of estimate based on experience and on the best information available. At times such estimates will prove wide of the mark, but usually they are such as to permit a "fair" value to be shown on the balance sheet.

Fixed assets also present problems. Though it is usually practicable to state the initial cost of items included under fixed assets, judgment often enters into a decision as to whether subsequent expenditures, such as for new parts or modifications, should be classified as costs of fixed assets to be written off over a period of years, or whether they should be absorbed at once as expenses of the current period.

The decision in such cases affects both the balance sheet and the income statement. Failure to capitalize additions to fixed assets results in understatement of income in the period of expenditure, and corresponding overstatement in subsequent years. Capitalizing expenditures representing maintenance or repairs has a contrary effect.

Moreover, accounting for fixed assets requires judgment in estimating suitable charges to income for depreciation. Here the probable useful life of the asset and the likelihood of obsolescence must be considered. Any significant failure in determining the proper provision for depreciation affects the fairness of the income statement as well as the net amount at which fixed assets are carried on the balance sheet.

Inventories are another item requiring the exercise of judgment. The value of no item in financial statements is so little susceptible to exact statement as inventories. Estimates as to condition, salability, and even market value, may vary greatly. The convention of "cost or market, whichever lower" may be applied in a variety of manners to produce quite different results. Even the count or measurement of items in the inventory cannot always be exact.

Income Statement

Financial statements are usually prepared on an accrual basis. That means the income statement includes, to the extent possible, all income of a business applicable to the period covered, regardless of whether or not such income is fully represented by cash received in the same period. In similar manner, the statement includes, to the extent practicable, all costs and expenses applicable to the period.

Those objectives cannot be achieved by simply adding up the cash receipts and disbursements for the period. For instance, income is in some cases applicable to periods other than that in which the sale is made and the proceeds received, the reason being that full performance is not then completed. An example of this is the receipt of payment for goods or services which are to be delivered in the future. By the same token, amounts paid out today may be applicable not only to current operations, but also to those of several years to come. That is the reason for writing fixed assets off over their useful life. On the other hand, costs incurred today may not be paid for until some future time. Such is the case when goods or services received today are to be paid for at a later date.

The preparation of the incoming statement thus involves one of the basic objectives of accounting — the matching of costs and expenses against income. In great measure, this is relatively simple but as to many items the problem cannot be solved by formula, and allocation of income or expenses between periods must rest on judgment.

Consolidated Statements

Many business organizations prepare financial statements showing the financial position and results of operations of the parent company and its subsidiaries as though they were a single business entity. These are called consolidated statements and usually include only those subsidiaries over which the parent company has control. As a general criterion, the existence of control over a subsidiary is determined by whether the parent company has more than 50% of the voting control, thereby giving it the power to direct, or to cause the direction of, the management and policies of the subsidiary.

Even though the power to control a subsidiary is present, consideration is also given to whether its inclusion or exclusion in the consolidated statements will fairly and realistically present the financial position and results of operations of the group of companies. The decision to include or exclude certain subsidiaries often requires the exercise of judgment; as, for example, when legal or geographical considerations affect the extent of the control exercised or when the operations of some subsidiaries are not similar or complementary to the operations of the consolidated group.

Although consolidated financial statements serve a very useful purpose, they have important limitations which require consideration. For example, the status of bondholders and other creditors and the respective assets against which their claims rank in priority will not usually be shown. Thus, consolidated statements may be inadequate for certain purposes unless accompanied by additional statements or footnotes. However, when substantially all the securities of a subsidiary are owned by the parent company and the subsidiary is, in effect, an operating division of an integrated business, the individual income and surplus statements of the parent company alone, or of the subsidiaries, would not ordinarily be significant. On the other hand, disclosure of the parent company's equity in the aggregate earnings or losses of unconsolidated subsidiaries is usually regarded as significant information in connection with financial statements. The equity of minority stockholders — i.e., those outside the group — in the earnings, capital stock, and surplus of subsidiary companies included in consolidated statements, is generally stated separately.

Consolidated statements are intended to show the position and results of operations on the basis of considering the entire consolidated group as a single unit. Hence, intercompany sales and intercompany profits not realized by means of sales outside the group are usually eliminated in consolidation. However, practical considerations may at times necessitate minor deviations from this rule.

The examples cited illustrate only a few of the areas in which judgment enters into the recording of business transactions and the preparation of financial statements.

Judgment Is Guided by Accounting Principles

One might question the usefulness of statements whose fairness rests so heavily upon judgment rather than upon demonstrated fact. But as against such doubts it should be borne in mind that the judgment employed is an informed one. It is concerned with actualties and does not descend to mere imagination. The statements reflect the considered judgment of prudent businessmen as to the proper interpretation of all the pertinent information relating to the transactions involved.

Furthermore, broad principles, known as generally accepted accounting principles, serve as guides in making accounting decisions. Those principles have been developed over the years as a result of study and experience in presenting useful financial information. They comprise a body of accounting conventions for dealing with problems such as those described. When financial statements are prepared in conformity with those principles, and are checked by CPAs, they almost always present financial facts fairly, even though approximations and estimates have been necessary.

It is not the purpose of this pamphlet to deal with accounting principles as such. Many excellent books are available to those who wish to pursue the subject further, and a series of *Accounting Research Bulletins* dealing with the application of those principles to a variety of specific problems has been issued by the committee on accounting procedure of the American Institute of Accountants.

Company Has Primary Responsibility for Financial Statements

There is one further point that should be understood before considering the following sections of this pamphlet. Financial statements are primarily the statements and representations of the company. The fact that they have been examined and reported upon by a CPA does not shift the company's responsibility for the fairness of the information presented.

The transactions with which the accounting records are concerned, and the recording of those transactions in the books, are matters within the direct or primary knowledge and control of the company. While the CPA may supervise the keeping of the records, and often prepare the financial statements, his knowledge of the transactions is a secondary one. Thus, even though the financial statements may reflect the influence of the CPA, the company in presenting them to others must be considered to have accepted, and adopted, the CPA's recommendations. The company cannot be excused for presenting statements which it knows to be false or misleading any more than can the CPA.

Section II: THE CPA's REPORT

The characteristics of the CPA's report depend upon the purpose for which the examination was undertaken. However, all reports based on audits whose objective is an opinion on the fairness of financial statements have characteristics in common. They include a description of the work done by the CPA and present his findings. In some instances, they include qualifications of the opinion, or an assertion that an opinion cannot be given. In such cases, an explanation of the conditions which make these necessary is included in the report. The CPA's representations are confined to and expressed in his report. It is essential, therefore, that users of financial statements read the CPA's report carefully to be fully informed as to the views the CPA holds regarding the fairness of the statements.

The report may take varying forms. In some cases, a detailed, or long-form, report is submitted. In other cases, the report is limited to a concise statement of the scope of the examination and the related opinion of the CPA concerning the financial statements. This is referred to as the short-form report.

Not infrequently, both types of reports are submitted: the long-form report being principally for the information of the management, or a small group of creditors; the short-form report being used in connection with financial statements submitted by the company to those whose concern is primarily with the over-all picture rather than with the details of the audit or the management of the business. The short-form report is customarily used in reporting upon financial statements to be published in reports to stockholders. Regardless of form, however, the CPA is careful to word his reports so that readers will not be led to place greater reliance upon them than is intended.

The CPA Expresses an Opinion

A word of caution is appropriate at this point. For many years, it was customary to introduce the CPA's opinion with the phrase "We certify that . . . " It is quite natural, therefore, that the opinion came to be known as a "certificate" — for the same reason, it became customary to say that the CPA "certified" financial statements. Nevertheless, the CPA's conclusions are essentially matters of opinion rather than of fact.

His opinion is an expression of personal judgment. In recognition of this, it is now customary to use the phrase "In our opinion," to introduce the conclusions set forth in the CPA's report as to the fairness of financial statements.

The opinion of a CPA is not comparable to the certificate of a weighmaster who certifies as to the weight of a load of goods. As explained, financial data often cannot be gauged by precise standards. The CPA is not an insurer. He cannot guarantee that the figures presented in financial statements are literally correct. It is not possible to certify the accuracy of management's judgment or estimates, but the opinion of an independent expert, skilled in analyzing and appraising the grounds upon which such decisions are made, is valuable to those who lack the opportunity, the time, or the training to make such an investigation themselves.

Since he must assume responsibility for his opinions, it is proper that the CPA should be the sole judge of his ability to express them. If, in his judgment, it is necessary or desirable to include explanations of his findings or to take exception to some aspect of the financial statements, those matters are usually included in a separate paragraph of the report. The CPA is responsible for reporting any exceptions clearly and unequivocally, whether they involve the scope of the audit work, particular items in the financial statements, the soundness of the company's accounting practices (as regards either the books or the financial statements) or lack of consistency in the application of accounting practices.

It bears repetition that the financial statements, with all supplemental descriptive and explanatory data, including footnotes, are regarded as representations of the company. It is upon all these representations that the CPA exercises his independent, considered judgment and renders his opinion. If explanations are essential or desirable, and they are not incorporated in the statements in a manner he considers satisfactory, he makes appropriate explanations in his report.

The Opinion May Be Expressed in a Short-Form Report

The short-form type of report, which outlines in general terms the scope of the examination made and states concisely the CPA's opinion regarding the fairness of the financial statements, is usually adequate for the needs of those who seek assurance primarily as to the over-all fairness of the presentation of a company's financial position and the results of its operations. The following wording of a short-form report, recommended by the committee on auditing procedure of the American Institute of Accountants in 1948, is typical:

> "We have examined the balance-sheet of X Company as of December 31, 19__ and the related statement(s) of income and surplus for the year then

ended. Our examination was made in accordance with generally accepted auditing standards, and accordingly included such tests of the accounting records and such other auditing procedures as we considered necessary in the circumstances.

"In our opinion, the accompanying balance-sheet and statement(s) of income and surplus present fairly the financial position of X Company at December 31, 19__, and the results of its operations for the year then ended, in conformity with generally accepted accounting principles applied on a basis consistent with that of the preceding year."[1]

The first paragraph sets forth the CPA's representations regarding the scope of his audit. It represents that the audit met the profession's standards for competence and workmanship. It also points out that, in observing generally accepted auditing standards, the CPA made all the tests and employed all other procedures which he considered necessary in the circumstances for an informed, professional opinion regarding the financial statements. A major portion of this pamphlet is devoted to explaining the CPA's approach to an examination and to outlining the ways in which he selects and applies auditing procedures.

The second paragraph deals with the CPA's findings. As noted previously, the CPA expresses an *opinion*. He does not *guarantee* that the statements are correct. He states that in his best judgment, based upon a careful audit, the financial statements set forth all the information necessary to present fairly the company's financial position and the results of its operations. He states further that, in his opinion, the statements are presented in conformity with generally accepted accounting principles, which were mentioned briefly in the early part of this pamphlet, and that those principles have been applied on a basis consistent with that of the preceding year.

The expression "presents fairly" should be noted particularly, because it constitutes the essence of the CPA's opinion. It indicates the belief that, although the amounts shown in the statements may not represent exactness, they are near enough to actuality (under generally accepted accounting principles) to be accepted as correct for practical purposes. Further, it stresses the CPA's belief that the method of presentation — that is, the arrangement of the items — is such as to give a truthful over-all picture of financial position and results of operations.

While this form of report has been recommended as a standard, it is not prescribed or recommended for invariable use. It is adaptable to the needs of the particular case. For example, the CPA may consider it desirable to expand the report to include a brief explanation of certain auditing procedures he has employed, or has not employed, or of certain

---

[1] Statements on Auditing Procedure No. 24, *Revision in Short-Form Accountant's Report or Certificate.*

accounting practices followed by the company. He may wish to include information which he believes is not adequately explained in the financial statements. As has been indicated, he may in some cases consider it necessary to qualify his opinion in certain respects, or to disclaim any opinion as to the over-all fairness of the financial statements. Variations from the standard wording should be carefully considered by users of the statements. They may be important.

The Opinion May Be Expressed in a Long-Form Report

The long-form report customarily outlines in some detail the work done and the CPA's conclusions regarding the more important matters. It usually includes comments on the company's operations and comparisons with previous periods. It may include a wide variety of information, such as statistics on changes in financial or working capital position, agings of receivables and payables, an application of funds statement, a summary of insurance coverage as taken from policies submitted for examination, and other information which may be appropriate in the particular circumstances.

It is not uncommon to find the wording of the short-form report, previously quoted, incorporated in the long-form report. Recommendations on internal control and accounting procedures are frequently submitted in a separate memorandum.

The long-form report is generally intended primarily for the use of management and, for that reason, may not accompany financial statements presented to outsiders. However, it is frequently submitted by the company to bankers and other credit grantors upon request. Credit grantors often find either the long-form report presented for management purposes, or a similar report designed specifically for their needs, to be of great value.

The CPA's Report May Be Qualified

Depending upon his findings, the CPA may express an unqualified opinion as to the over-all fairness of the presentation of the financial data; he may express an opinion qualified in some respects; or he may feel that no opinion is justified under the circumstances.

If he is completely satisfied that the financial statements present fairly the financial position and results of operations, the CPA usually expresses an unqualified opinion to that effect. The short-form report previously quoted is an example of an unqualified report. When the CPA has not been completely satisfied on some point, or when he feels that some part of the financial position or results is not fairly presented, but under the circumstances the matter in question is not of sufficient significance to prohibit the expression of an opinion on the statements taken as a whole, he may express a qualified opinion, indicating the nature of the reservation or exception.

In general, the necessity for expressing a qualified opinion occurs when the CPA has not been able to make an examination sufficiently complete to warrant the expression of an unqualified opinion or when he has found violations of accepted accounting principles which the company is unwilling to correct. When either of these situations exists, the CPA weighs their significance and importance. If the statements read in the light of his qualifications permit a reasonable appraisal of the financial position and results of operations, he expresses a qualified opinion.

It is not possible to prepare standard wording for use in expressing a qualified opinion; the circumstances calling for qualified opinions are far too numerous and varied and must be dealt with as they arise. However, the following examples illustrate the manner in which they appear in CPAs' reports. The first example shows wording that might be used when certain auditing procedures normally considered necessary were omitted. The second involves an exception to the company's accounting practices. The third concerns a reservation because of uncertainty as to a contingent liability. The fourth illustrates an exception with respect to consistency in the application of accounting principles:

(I)

"Records supporting the changes in the inventories at one of the divisions between the date of the last physical inventory, October 31, 19___, and the end of the company's accounting year, December 31, 19___, were not completed and in proper order for satisfactory examination. The auditing tests and observations made by us indicate the possibility that a further reduction might have been found necessary. This reduction would not, in our opinion, exceed $_____.

"In our opinion, subject to the exception with respect to inventories explained above, ..."

(II)

"In our opinion, except that no provision was made for net losses, estimated to be approximately $_____, on purchase commitments, ..."

(III)

"In our opinion, except as to such adjustments as may result from final determination of taxes on income, ..."

(IV)

"As stated in the notes to the financial statements, the company changed its method of computing depreciation, effective January 1, 19___. This change, which we approve, resulted in an increase of $_____ in the depreciation provision for the year and a corresponding decrease in net income for the year.

"In our opinion, . . . present fairly . . . in conformity with generally accepted accounting principles applied on a basis consistent with that of the preceding year, except for the change in the method of computing depreciation referred to in the preceding paragraph."

The CPA May Disclaim an Opinion

The CPA refrains from expressing either an unqualified opinion or one that is qualified when, because of limitations on the scope of his audit or departures from generally accepted accounting principles, his exceptions or reservations would be such as to destroy the significance of the opinion on the statements taken as a whole. In such cases, the CPA is obliged to indicate that he is not in a position to express an opinion on the over-all fairness of the financial statements and to give his reasons why. He may, if he considers it appropriate, express an opinion limited to those parts of the financial statements with which he is satisfied. When he does so, however, he first makes it absolutely clear that he is not expressing an opinion on the over-all fairness of the financial statements.[2]

As in the case of qualified opinions, it is not possible to suggest any standard wording that would be applicable generally for the disclaimer of an opinion. However, the following paragraph illustrates the type of language that might be incorporated in the CPA's report in such cases:

> "The terms of our engagement did not include the verification of accounts receivable by direct correspondence, nor did it include the physical observation or price tests of inventories, and we did not satisfy ourselves in regard to these assets by other means. Nothing came to our attention during the examination which would indicate thát these items are not stated fairly. However, in view of the materiality of these assets, we are unable to express an opinion on the over-all representations in the attached statements."

It should be remembered that the CPA is not in a position to force his client to authorize a satisfactory audit. If the client is unwilling to have the CPA make an examination of sufficient scope to justify expressing an opinion on the over-all fairness of the financial statements, the CPA must state clearly in his report the limitations of his audit and the degree of responsibility which its scope justifies.

Section III: AUDITING PHILOSOPHY

The general misunderstanding as to the real significance of financial statements also extends to the audit of those statements by CPAs. People who mistakenly suppose that statements represent financial facts expressed in exact figures quite naturally assume that an audit of such statements can be nothing but an exact and complete verification of the figures on the statements.

Objectives of Audit

The objectives of an audit require no such lengthy and microscopic scrutiny. What they do require is sufficient examination of the state-

2 Statements on Auditing Procedure No. 23 (Revised), *Clarification of Accountant's Report when Opinion Is Omitted.*

ments and supporting records, and sufficient study of the company's accounting practices, to place the CPA in a position to express an informed opinion upon the general fairness of the statements. An examination for that purpose does not ordinarily require an exhaustive investigation of details of the company's operations.

The soundness of accounting judgments and estimates depends upon the integrity and competence of those who make them and upon their adherence to generally accepted accounting principles. It is for an independent review of the reasonableness of both management's and employees' decisions regarding these questions, even more than for tests of the mathematical accuracy of the accounting data, that an unbiased, objective audit, as provided by CPAs, is desirable. The objectives of an audit, in modern practice, are much broader in scope than the discovery of mathematical errors or the detection of defalcations or fraud.

Of course, the testing of the accounting records and supporting information is important — in fact, it is a necessary part of the process of forming an opinion regarding the soundness of the management's accounting decisions and the integrity of the accounts. Moreover, while the usual audit which is undertaken to enable the CPA to express an opinion on the financial statements may not be relied upon to disclose minor defalcations or fraud, it is incumbent upon the CPA to be alert to the possibilities of irregularities and to inform the management about weaknesses in internal control which come to his attention and which conceivably could permit such irregularities to remain undisclosed.

CPA's Approach to Audit

CPAs satisfy themselves as to the general fairness of financial statements:

1. By a general review of the accounts and records and comparison of the figures shown on the statements with the sources from which they are drawn.
2. By a study of the accounting procedures regularly followed by the company and consideration of any departures from those practices.
3. By independent sampling tests (through inspection, correspondence, or other means) of the existence of assets.
4. By the application of various audit tests to determine, so far as reasonably possible, that all liabilities are reflected in the balance sheet in actual or approximate amounts.
5. By analyses, tests, and over-all review of the income and expense accounts.
6. By test-procedures designed to determine the authenticity and general correctness of the accounts on which the statements are based.

Audits Are Not Uniform

Each audit discloses circumstances which require differences to a greater or lesser degree in the auditing procedures that should be employed, the manner in which they should be used, and the extent to which they should be applied. Among the reasons for these differences in requirements are that: (1) significant variations exist in the nature and scope of the operations of companies in different industrial or commercial groups, or even of companies within the same group or classification; (2) the degree of effectiveness of the internal control varies among companies; (3) even within a single company the operating and accounting problems frequently change from year to year; and (4) the amount of detail to be included in the financial statements varies. In new engagements, there may be the additional problem of making an appropriate review of the important transactions of prior years and determining the nature and extent of the accounting procedures and internal control in effect.

These differences make it apparent that it is impossible to lay down specific procedures which could be applied satisfactorily in all cases. Often there is a choice of procedures, any of which would be satisfactory in a given situation. Here, as elsewhere in accounting and auditing, there must be an exercise of judgment based upon experience and upon a clear view of the objective of providing a sound basis for an informed, professional opinion.

The CPA Usually Relies Upon Tests

In most audits, investigation of every transaction would not only be excessively costly — it is also unnecessary. The CPA bases his examination upon tests of the records and upon inspection of selected transactions.

The extent of testing in any audit is decided by the CPA in the light of his best independent judgment as to the amount required to constitute a fair sampling of the record being tested. In deciding upon the character of the tests to be made, and the extent to which they should be applied, one of the most important factors taken into consideration is the system of internal control. When evidence exists that the system is effective, the CPA properly concludes that the accounting records and supporting data have a higher degree of dependability than would otherwise be the case, and limits his testing accordingly. However, when his investigation shows that the system has points of weakness, he extends the scope of his testing. If the internal control is considered grossly inadequate or ineffective, he may feel compelled to review the entries in considerable detail before he can express an informed opinion on the financial statements.

Other factors which enter into the planning of tests include the materiality of the item to be tested and the relative risk of the existence of irregularities. Thus, for example, where office supplies are a relatively minor item on the financial statements, they would not usually be investigated extensively. On the other hand, certain kinds of assets, such as cash, marketable securities, negotiable papers, et cetera, are obviously of such a nature that the risk of irregularities is relatively greater. The CPA usually requires more conclusive evidence for items of that type than for others, even though they may not be as material in relation to the over-all picture as some items regarding which less exhaustive tests are suitable.

The CPA must defer final determination of his procedures until he has a dependable understanding of the available evidence and has judged its reliability. Although he may prepare a tentative program of procedures to be employed in a particular audit, using as a basis the results of his preliminary investigations, he must at all times be prepared to revise the program if in the course of his work he finds that changes are necessary.

The CPA Often Performs Part of the Audit During the Year

The CPA frequently performs much of his audit work prior to the close of the annual period. For example, he may make interim or periodic audits for the purpose of reporting on financial statements for portions of the year. If the CPA intends to express an opinion regarding the overall fairness of the interim financial statements, he observes the same standards and the same care in the selection and application of his auditing procedures as he would with respect to annual statements.[8] However, the closer contact and greater familiarity with the business gained by periodic interim examinations may make it unnecessary to carry through in as complete detail for the interim periods all of the procedures customarily applied to the year-end statements.

CPAs often carry out important phases of their audit work as of an interim date even though they will render a report only with respect to year-end financial statements. The choice of the procedures employed, and the extent to which they are applied at such interim dates, depend very largely upon the company's internal control. For that reason, a considerable part of the interim work may first be directed to determining the effectiveness of the company's system of internal control. If the internal control is effective, a major portion of the work on inventories, plant accounts, cash and receivables, for example, may in many cases be accomplished more satisfactorily during the year than is possible after the close of the year. Some of the work must of necessity be held over until the later date, and the CPA reviews the transactions taking place during the intervening period to assure himself that nothing out of the ordinary has occurred.

The practice of doing much of the audit work during the year is of advantage to the company as well as to the CPA. One of the most im-

[8] Statements on Auditing Procedure No. 8, *Interim Financial Statements and the Auditor's Report Thereon.*

portant advantages is that the CPA can familiarize himself with the operations of the company at an earlier date. This enables him to bring any undesirable features of the company's accounting practices to the management's attention promptly for remedial action. Moreover, by doing much of the detailed work at a time when the pressure for issuing the financial statements is not so great, the CPA is generally able to work with less inconvenience to the company's staff.

The CPA Is Guided by Auditing Standards

It is apparent that to weigh the reasonableness of management's accounting decisions and to express an informed, professional opinion regarding them, the CPA himself must exercise sound judgment. This responsibility demands the highest standards of competence and integrity.

Various professional organizations, such as the American Institute of Accountants, as well as state societies of certified public accountants, and state and Federal governmental bodies, over the years have developed, clarified, and vitalized standards which guide CPAs in their work.[4]

These standards are the underlying principles of auditing which govern the nature and extent of the evidence to be obtained by means of auditing procedures. They are broad in scope and concern both the CPA's personal qualifications and the quality of his work. Whereas auditing procedures must be varied to meet the requirements of the particular engagement, standards to be observed in selecting and applying the procedures are the same in all circumstances.

Personal Standards

Generally accepted auditing standards require the CPA to be proficient in accounting and auditing; he must have the training and experience necessary to perform any engagement he undertakes in a professional manner.

The most widely recognized evidence that a person has attained this standard of competence is his possession of the right to call himself a Certified Public Accountant. As stated previously, this right is granted by each state to any person who can demonstrate that he possesses the requisite character, education, and training, and can pass a professional examination.

Practically all states use examinations prepared by the American Institute of Accountants to test the applicant's mastery of his subject. To pass these examinations the applicant must have completed a rigorous course of training involving instruction in the theory and practice of accounting,

[4] See *Auditing Standards — Their Generally Accepted Significance and Scope.* — Special report by committee on auditing procedure (American Institute of Accountants, 1947).

auditing and commercial law, and must have acquired experience in dealing with practical accounting problems. After becoming a CPA, the practicing auditor must continue to keep abreast of current developments in accounting and auditing techniques.

Independence, both historically and philosophically, is the foundation of the public accounting profession. The CPA must not only possess extensive technical skill; he must also maintain the highest standards of honest, objective judgment and consideration. Independence is one of his most important personal qualifications.

Independence is an attitude of mind much deeper than the surface display of visible standards. The standards may change or become more exacting, but the quality itself remains unchanged. Rules of conduct cannot of themselves, therefore, assure independence. They can, however, provide objective standards to guide the CPA in all his professional endeavors.

The rules of professional conduct adopted by the American Institute of Accountants [5] and by the various state societies of certified public accountants are designed to maintain the high standards of independence which the work of the CPA requires. Typically, the rules provide penalties for false and misleading statements, and prohibit contingent fees, financial interest in clients' affairs, occupations incompatible with public accounting, commissions, brokerage, and fee splitting — all intended to avoid even the possible appearance that the CPA's judgment may have been wrongly influenced.

The CPA's personal standards also demand the exercise of due professional care in the performance of his work. Due care involves not only the employment of procedures which are proper under the circumstances of a case, but also the proper application and co-ordination of the procedures employed. He must observe due care both in his field work and in reporting his findings.

Standards of Field Work

To meet generally accepted auditing standards regarding the performance of his field work, the CPA's work must be adequately planned and his assistants, if any, must be properly supervised. Proper planning is an essential prerequisite of good audit work. It is particularly important in connection with the auditing of inventories and is indispensable to the achievement of satisfactory co-ordination in auditing procedures. Closely related to proper planning is the necessity for critical review by the accounting firm's supervisory personnel of the work and decisions of those whose skill and experience are less extensive.

[5] These are discussed at some length in *Professional Ethics of Public Accounting* by John L. Carey (American Institute of Accountants, 1946).

Professional standards of field work also require the CPA to make a proper study of the existing internal control and to evaluate its effectiveness by positive tests designed to demonstrate its substance as well as its form.[6] The adequacy of the system of internal control, which from the CPA's viewpoint concerns primarily the measures adopted by the business to safeguard its assets and to check the reliability and accuracy of its accounting data, is of vital importance in the selection and application of appropriate audit procedures.

Standards of Reporting

In his report, the CPA states whether the financial statements are presented in accordance with generally accepted accounting principles and whether the principles have been consistently observed during the current period in relation to the preceding period. The CPA's responsibility relates not only to the propriety of that which is set forth, but also to the inclusion of such additional information as may be necessary to make the statements not misleading. If disclosures in the financial statements relating to items of material importance are not reasonably adequate, he clarifies these matters in his report.[7]

Section IV: AUDITING PROCEDURES

The preceding discussion was directed primarily to the broader considerations involved in an audit — what was called the philosophy of auditing. The rest of this pamphlet deals with some of the ways in which the philosophy may be reflected in the selection and application of auditing procedures.[8] The discussion is of necessity very general because, as already explained, auditing procedures must vary with the circumstances. More detailed and comprehensive illustrations of the application of auditing procedures are presented in the series of *Case Studies in Auditing Procedure,* issued by the committee on auditing procedure of the American Institute of Accountants. Each of those case studies describes the auditing procedures which were actually followed in a particular case.

---

6 *Internal Control — Elements of a Co-ordinated System and its Importance to Management and the Independent Public Accountant* — Special report by committee on auditing procedure (American Institute of Accountants, 1949). The committee is also sponsoring a series of three *Case Studies in Internal Control* to illustrate the manner in which accountants reviewed internal control and applied their findings in actual engagements.

7 A summary of references to disclosure in various Institute publications appeared in the August 1948 issue of *The Journal of Accountancy* as "Disclosure in Financial Statements — Codification of Institute Pronouncements," pp. 112-118.

8 Certain aspects of this subject are discussed in the series of *Statements an Auditing Procedure* issued by the committee on auditing procedure of the American Institute of Accountants.

Audit Techniques

Although the nature of the techniques employed by CPAs should be readily apparent from the discussion of procedures which follows, a brief description of them, in general terms, may be helpful.

Analysis and Review: The principal means by which the CPA forms his opinion as to the fairness of financial statements is through careful analysis and critical review of the data presented, with a view to appraising whether they appear to be reasonable and reliable. This process is applied not only to the company's data, but also to data accumulated by the CPA himself in the course of his audit. One way this is accomplished is by the comparison of balances in the trial balance at the balance-sheet date with those in the trial balance at the end of the previous comparable period, noting for investigation any items which appear to be out of line with previous experience. Another comparison is that of the gross profit percentage during the current period with the corresponding percentages in previous periods. A somewhat different approach is to break down the detail of individual accounts so that any unusual items requiring special investigation may be identified or so that the more significant transactions in the account may be selected for investigation as a part of the testing program.

Observation: The CPA should, of course, be observant at all times. However, the term "observation," as used in auditing, refers to the practice of being present to observe the manner in which various procedures of the company are being performed by its employees. In particular, it is used in reference to the CPA's attendance at the counting of the inventory. In the course of his audit, the CPA may also observe the company's procedures in the handling of cash and in the operation of other phases of its system of internal control.

Inspection: A large part of the CPA's work involves the inspection of physical assets, and of documents and other evidence supporting the figures in the accounting records. This process includes such procedures as counting cash on hand, testing inventory counts and visiting plants to gain general familiarity with the company's facilities and operations. It also includes such steps as examining invoices, checks, and other documents supporting entries in the books, and reading the minutes of stockholders' and directors' meetings for information on actions authorized by those groups.

Confirmation: In numerous phases of the audit, the CPA obtains confirmation of items shown on the records by advice directly from the individual or company in a position to verify such items. For example, the CPA generally obtains reports as to the balances in the bank accounts at the balance-sheet date directly from the banks in which the company's funds are deposited. Confirmation requests are similarly sent to customers of the company on a test basis. In this way, the CPA receives confirmation of certain information from persons or businesses that are independent of the company under examination. Requests for confirmation are mailed personally by the CPA in envelopes bearing his return address and are usually accompanied by a return envelope addressed to the CPA.

Inquiry: The CPA generally secures considerable information by discussing with officers and employees of the company various questions that arise during the audit. These inquiries generally involve points which are not completely clear from the records, matters of general company policy, or such items as contingent liabilities regarding which information can often be supplied only by the management. Not infrequently, the more important of these explanations are reduced to writing in a statement signed by responsible officers of the company.[9]

Computation: The CPA also does a considerable amount of work independently testing arithmetical calculations and computing such figures as depreciation, interest accrued, amortization of bond discount, tax liabilities, et cetera.

Auditing Procedures Often Employed

Some of the procedures often employed by CPAs in the audits of small or medium-sized companies engaged in industry or trading are described in the following pages. The procedures are discussed in relation to the principal items usually appearing in financial statements of corporations. However, the general approach would be the same in the case of a partnership or proprietorship.

It should be understood that the procedures would seldom be performed in the order presented here. In practice the procedures are coordinated to deal with related items (e.g., sales and receivables).

It is not considered practicable to present in this pamphlet descriptions of procedures as they might be employed in the audits of large business units because of the complexities of their operations and accounting procedures. Nor are the special problems that arise in certain audits such as those of insurance companies, brokerage concerns, banks and trust companies, municipalities, clubs, hospitals, colleges and universities, or other nonprofit enterprises, considered here. However, the broad objectives and the basic considerations involved in such audits are the same as those involved in the audits of manufacturing and mercantile organizations.

In the case of certain items in the financial statements, the CPA makes an extensive investigation. In other instances, he proceeds only far enough to satisfy himself that the items cannot be incorrect to any great extent. As explained earlier, the materiality of the item and the risk of

9 Statements on Auditing Procedure No. 4, *Clients' Written Representations Regarding Inventories, Liabilities and Other Matters.*

its being incorrectly stated in the particular instance, together with the effectiveness of the company's system of internal control, enter into his decision as to how far he should go in verifying each item on the financial statements. It should be remembered that the CPA cannot achieve absolute certainty. To approach it would require verification of every transaction — a process which would generally be far more expensive than the result would justify.

Many of the procedures described are applicable in most audits. Others are not always applicable. Still others, not discussed here, are necessary at times. Accordingly, in reading the following pages, it is important to bear in mind that, as stated before, each audit must be designed to fit the particular circumstances. The discussion which follows does not constitute a "standard audit program." It does not describe a "typical audit." This pamphlet does not tell a person how to make an audit; nor does it present a yardstick for weighing the adequacy of an audit. It is the CPA's responsibility, and his alone, to determine what procedures are necessary and how extensively they shall be applied in a particular audit.

Cash

Cash includes such items as amounts on deposit in banks, undeposited receipts, change and other working funds, and petty cash funds. Because of the relative ease with which errors or irregularities can occur in the handling and recording of cash, an effective system of internal control over the handling and recording of cash is of the utmost importance.

The CPA's examination of cash is designed to afford a reasonable basis for his opinion that cash, as stated on the balance sheet, is available without restriction, or with restrictions as indicated. The detection of embezzlement or kindred frauds was once a primary purpose of an examination by a CPA but, as the size of business organizations and the number of transactions have increased, with consequent improvement in internal controls, this purpose has become less important and the usual examination is no longer designed primarily to disclose such irregularities. The present-day aim of auditing procedures for cash is comparable to those for the examination of other assets — to state the amount fairly but not necessarily precisely.

In small or medium-sized companies, the circumstances do not always permit the development of as effective a system of internal control as is obtainable in large business units. It follows that the audits of many smaller business units require relatively more extensive application of auditing procedures.

Cash in Banks

Each bank with which the company does business is asked to confirm the balances in the company's bank accounts at the balance-sheet date.

A special confirmation form has been developed to assist the banks in answering these requests.[10] In addition to asking for confirmation of balances in the accounts, the request form provides for information regarding such important matters as restrictions on withdrawal of funds, direct or contingent liabilities to the bank, such as loans or discounted notes, and any of the company's assets held as collateral.

Balances of cash on deposit as reported by banks, seldom agree with the corresponding balances recorded in the company's records because of such items as checks issued by the company that have not been paid by the banks, or deposits in transit. To satisfy himself that these reconciling items are in order, the CPA usually compares them with the books and with bank statements and canceled checks received by him directly from the bank subsequent to the date of the reconcilation. If the bank statements are not received directly from the bank, the CPA usually proves them by ascertaining that the total of the opening balance and deposits, according to the bank statement, less the sum of the accompanying checks, equals the closing balance shown on the bank statement. In the case of large deposits in transit, authenticated deposit slips are usually obtained from the banks and compared with the books, item by item.

Cash on Hand

In satisfying himself as to cash on hand, the CPA usually counts it, making sure that no item such as vouchers for disbursements of significant amounts made prior to the balance-sheet date, or checks which do not appear to be readily collectible, are included in the cash funds. He also satisfies himself that the amounts of all cash funds, as determined by his counts, are in agreement with the books, and that all receipts produced as a part of the cash balance have been entered in the cash book prior to the close of the period. Where the company has a number of small petty cash accounts, it may not be necessary to count them all. In such cases, the CPA frequently requests confirmations of the amounts from the custodians of the funds.

The CPA, in counting cash, takes precautions against temporary substitution from other funds or from other sources. To accomplish this, he may secure control over the other funds and negotiable assets until the count is completed. Control may be obtained in many cases by providing that no one may have access to the items unless accompanied by the CPA, or by sealing the containers in which the items are kept.

Cash Transactions

To satisfy himself that cash receipts and disbursements have been correctly recorded, the CPA usually selects a sample period or periods for

10 Standard Bank Confirmation Form — 1940, available from American Institute of Accountants.

checking cash transactions in detail. The procedures applied generally include examination of checks issued by the company during the sample period, and paid by the bank, to see that they appear to be bona fide checks issued for bona fide business purposes to bona fide payees, and comparison of the checks with the cash disbursements records and with supporting evidence. Receipts, as shown by the cash receipts records, are traced to the bank statements, to duplicate deposit slips, or to other documents which support the records of the disposition made of them. As an over-all check, to be sure that all recorded receipts and disbursements have been accounted for, total cash receipts and disbursements, as shown by the company's records, may be reconciled with total deposits and withdrawals during the sample period, as shown by the bank statements.

CPAs usually obtain bank statements covering a short period immediately following the balance-sheet date to examine returned checks for evidence of post-dating or failure to enter withdrawals in the cash records for the period ended on the balance-sheet date. These "cut-off" statements also enable the CPA to trace deposits in transit at that time to the bank statements and to satisfy himself as to whether any items have been returned. The bank statements are usually obtained by the CPA directly from the bank. If they are not, the CPA proves them in the manner previously outlined.

Notes Receivable

The business under review may have several different types of notes receivable among its assets. It may have notes receivable, including installment notes, arising out of its regular business with its customers. There may be notes receivable from affiliated concerns or from stockholders, directors, officers, or employees. There may also be notes receivable arising from other transactions outside the ordinary business of the company. Some of these notes may have been discounted, in which case the company may have a contingent liability.

The objectives of the CPA in auditing notes receivable are to satisfy himself that the items making up the amounts on the balance sheet are genuine and that they are stated at amounts they may reasonably be expected to realize. He also satisfies himself that they are properly classified on the balance sheet, with the different types shown separately, if significant, and that none has been pledged, sold, assigned, or discounted, except as disclosed in the statements.

Notes on hand are usually examined and the details compared with the company's records. Any evidence of collateral may also be examined to determine whether the collateral appears adequate or whether provision should be made for possible loss.

It is generally accepted auditing procedure, where practicable and reasonable, to ask the makers of the notes to confirm the balances payable and the collateral pledged, if any.[11] If the notes are numerous, the confirmation procedure may be performed on a test basis. Replies to these confirmation requests are checked to the records and any differences are investigated. As was indicated under "Cash," the bank confirmation form provides for information as to notes discounted with banks. When notes are in the hands of attorneys or others for collection, confirmation that the notes are being held for the account of the company is usually requested.

The CPA customarily reviews the records of notes receivable and analyzes the accounts to satisfy himself that the notes are being recorded properly. In addition to comparing the results of his count and the confirmations with the records, this analysis and review may also include consideration on a test basis of whether collections of principal and interest during the period under review have been recorded properly, and whether any notes have been sold, assigned, or discounted.

Accounts Receivable

Accounts receivable, like notes receivable, may arise from various types of transactions and, as in the case of notes receivable, the CPA's objective is to satisfy himself that they are presented fairly in appropriate detail. Since accounts receivable are generally related closely to sales, the CPA's audit of accounts receivable often plays an important part in his audit of income.

General

Unless the accounts receivable are few in number, the records of individual accounts are usually kept in a separate ledger, or ledgers, the total balances of which are "controlled" by summary accounts in the general ledger. It is customary, therefore, to obtain trial balances (a listing of balances) of the accounts in the subsidiary ledgers, making sure that the details on the trial balances are in agreement with the balances in the individual accounts and that the totals are in agreement with the general ledger.

The accounts may, at the same time, be scrutinized for unusually large items, or for items which for other reasons appear to require special investigation. If there are significant credit balances in any individual

11 Statements on Auditing Procedure No. 1, *Extensions of Auditing Procedure.* (American Institute of Accountants, 1939.)

accounts, they are investigated to see if they should be reclassified as liabilities for balance-sheet purposes.

Past-Due Items

The trial balances of accounts receivable, in addition to showing the balance due on each account, are often prepared so as to show the "aging" of the individual accounts. For example, the balance of each account may be analyzed to show the portion of the balance that is current and the portions that are thirty days, sixty days, ninety days, and over ninety days, past due. The calculation of this schedule is tested by comparison with the customer's accounts to assure its correctness, if the CPA has not prepared it himself.

Steps are also taken to see that adequate provision is made for material items which are in dispute, or which may not for other reasons be collected in full. For example, a customer may be making regular payments on his current account while old items in dispute are carried forward. It is customary to pay particular heed to the possible existence of such items when comparing the trial balance with the individual accounts. The aging schedule provides considerable assistance in this respect because it so readily directs attention to items past due.

The CPA usually discusses with the credit department, or with some responsible officer, disputed items and accounts and notes that are past due. On the basis of this discussion, and such other investigations of correspondence, loss experience, et cetera, as are deemed necessary to form an opinion regarding the collectibilty of the accounts and notes, the CPA satisfies himself as to whether sufficient allowance for probable losses from doubtful accounts and notes has been made. In the balance sheet, these estimates of possible losses are usually shown as deductions from the corresponding assets, or from the total of the receivables to which they relate if the estimates are combined in a single amount.

Allowances to Customers

The CPA customarily investigates the company's practice regarding the granting of trade discounts, cash discounts, and freight allowances. He may also make inquiries as to the existence of customers' claims for reduction in prices and for allowances on account of defective material or special quantity discounts. Recognition of such items in the financial statements is similar to that given estimates of bad debt losses, though it is not customary to disclose them separately.

Goods Consigned Out

If the company consigns goods to customers or agents or holds goods under orders from customers for future delivery, title not having passed to the customers, the CPA makes inquiries and reviews the records to satisfy himself that such items have not been improperly included in accounts receivable. They are ordinarily carried in the inventory at the inventory price.

Confirmation

As with notes receivable, accepted practice requires the CPA to obtain confirmation of a representative portion of the balances of accounts receivable by communicating directly with the debtors wherever practicable and reasonable, and where the aggregate amount of accounts receivable represents a significant portion of the current assets or the total assets of the company.[12] Experience has demonstrated that this procedure is generally practicable and reasonable and is the most satisfactory method of substantiating receivables. It should be noted, however, that the principal purposes of such confirmations are to establish the genuineness of the receivables, the proper recording of receipts and the accuracy of the balances, and to test the internal control, rather than to determine the debtor's credit worthiness.

The method, the extent, and the time of confirming receivables in each engagement, and whether all receivables, or a part of them, should be confirmed, are determined by the CPA in the light of the particular circumstances. In general, there are tw methods: the positive method and the negative method.

Method of Confirmation

When the postive method is used, the debtor is asked to reply directly to the CPA, stating whether the balance shown by the request is correct and, if not, the balance he considers correct. He is also asked to furnish information which may be of assistance in locating any difference. Under the negative method, the debtor is asked to reply only if the balance is incorrect.[13] The confirmation request is often in the form of a special letter, or of a sticker attached to the regular periodic statement, or it may be imprinted on the statement by a rubber stamp.

Extent of Confirmation

In addition to applying his judgment as to the method of confirming accounts receivable, the CPA must also decide whether under the circumstances a limited test will be satisfactory, or whether requests should be made for confirmation of a relatively large number, or even all, of the

---

12 Statements on Auditing Procedure No. 1, *Extensions of Auditing Procedure.*

13 Statements on Auditing Procedure No. 19, *Confirmation of Receivables (Postive and Negative Methods).*

accounts. In reaching a decision, he takes into consideration such factors as the type of business and the effectiveness of the internal control.

Some companies, such as public utilities and department stores, have a large number of accounts with small individual balances. Other companies have a much smaller number of accounts but individual balances may be large. If the company has a large number of accounts with small balances, and the internal control is good, the likelihood that the receivables may be materially misstated is slight. The CPA may, therefore, request confirmations for only a relatively small proportion of the accounts. It is not uncommon to use the negative method in such cases.[14] On the other hand, if the company has a smaller number of accounts, but with large individual balances, it is customary to confirm a relatively larger proportion of the accounts and to use the positive method.

It is often desirable to use both methods of confirmation in the same audit, confirming the more important accounts by the positive method and the remainder by the negative method.

Checking Results

Even when the positive method is adopted, it is usually impossible to secure responses to all requests. The percentage of replies varies considerably according to the type of customer with which the organization deals. The CPA must, therefore, decide whether the nature and extent of the response, taken in conjunction with his other auditing procedures, constitute a satisfactory basis for his opinion as to the receivables. Generally, the CPA reaches a decision in this respect by comparing the aggregate dollar amount confirmed with the aggregate dollar amount for which confirmations were requested, taking into account also the nature of the replies and the situations disclosed. If the CPA does not consider the results satisfactory, he pursues the matter further, either by communicating again with those who have not replied or by adopting alternative procedures, to satisfy himself that accounts with respect to which replies have not been received are in order.

When the internal control and other conditions warrant, the confirmation of accounts receivable and the general review of the accounts receivable records are frequently done as of an interim date.

Confirmation Omitted

Although confirmation of accounts receivable is generally practicable and reasonable, circumstances occasionally arise under which it is not.

[14] Statements on Auditing Procedure No. 3, *Inventories and Receivables of Department Stores, Installment Houses, Chain Stores and Other Retailers,* and No. 14, *Confirmation of Public Utility Accounts Receivable.*

The CPA may be able, in some cases, to satisfy himself by other, special auditing procedures which are substantially the equivalent of confirmation in the circumstances. If unable to do so, and the amount involved is sufficiently material, he must refrain from expressing an opinion. In any case, the fact that receivables were not confirmed must, if they are material, be disclosed in his report even though he has satisfied himself sufficiently by other auditing procedures.[15]

Inventory

Inventory consists of goods awaiting sale (the merchandise of a trading concern and the finished goods of a manufacturer), goods in the course of production (work in process), and goods to be consumed directly or indirectly in production (raw materials and supplies).[16]

The CPA's procedures are designed to satisfy him that the amounts set forth by the company as inventory represent actual inventory, that they are presented with reasonable accuracy and in accordance with generally accepted accounting principles consistently applied, and that the bases of stating the inventory, as well as the pledge or assignment of any inventory, are properly disclosed. These objectives require the CPA to investigate the care and accuracy with which the company has counted the inventory, the methods and bases adopted by the company in pricing it, and the substantial correctness of the company's mathematical computations.

Observation

To satisfy himself that the counting of the inventory is done carefully and accurately, and also to gain general familiarity with the inventory, the CPA is required by generally accepted auditing practice to be present at the inventory-taking to observe the effectiveness of the count procedures when it is practicable and reasonable to do so and the amount of the inventory is significant.[17] Although the CPA may review and approve the instructions for taking the inventory, and may test the count of some items, it is the company's responsibility to make the count satisfactorily. The CPA's purpose in observing the count is to satisfy himself that the company is discharging that responsibility. It should be clearly understood that the CPA does not hold himself out as an appraiser, valuer, or

---

15 Statements on Auditing Procedure No. 12, *Amendment to Extensions of Auditing Procedure.*

16 Accounting Research Bulletin No. 29, *Inventory Pricing,* and No. 30, *Current Assets and Current Liabilities — Working Capital.*

17 Statements on Auditing Procedure No. 1, *Extensions of Auditing Procedure,* and No. 16, *Case Studies on Inventories.*

expert in materials. He does not "take," "determine," or "supervise" the inventory.

Although many companies count the inventory at, or very close to, the end of the accounting period, it is not uncommon to do this at other dates. For example, some companies maintain a book (or card) record of the inventory on hand from day to day, called a perpetual inventory record. These companies sometimes check these book records by comparing actual counts of individual items with the records, adjusting the records for the differences disclosed, on a continuous basis throughout the year. They may not count the whole inventory at any one time. Other companies take the whole inventory at one time, but at a date other than the balance-sheet date.

Planning Observation

It is apparent that the CPA must plan his audit program carefully if he is to perform his procedures in connection with the inventory count efficiently and satisfactorily. In particular, this involves careful study of the company's inventory-taking instructions to its employees. When the counts are made during the year, it also involves proper consideration of the effectiveness of the book or perpetual inventory records and of the system of internal control to determine whether the CPA may plan to rely upon a general review of the records for transactions taking place between the dates when he observes the counting and the close of the period under review.

Outside Custodians

In addition to the stocks of inventory on their own premises, companies may also have inventories in public warehouses or with other outside custodians. Under these circumstances, the CPA usually requests confirmation of the nature and amounts of the inventory from the outside custodians. If the amounts involved represent a significant proportion of the current assets or of the total assets of the company, supplemental inquires may be made. At times, it may be necessary to make test counts of such inventories as well as those on the company's premises.

Observations Omitted

Although observation of physical stock-taking is a generally accepted auditing procedure, it is occasionally impracticable or unreasonable to perform it. The question then arises whether the CPA can give an informed opinion on the financial statements. In some rare cases, he may be able to adopt other, special auditing procedures which he feels give sufficient assurance as to the reliability of the inventory amounts to permit the expression of an opinion. If not, and the amounts involved are material, he must refrain from expressing an opinion. However, regardless of whether or not he has satisfied himself by other auditing procedures, the CPA must explain in his report that the counting of the inventory was not observed.[18]

Inventory Pricing

Although the procedures by which the CPA satisfies himself as to the fairness of the count are important, they are but one part of his audit of the inventories. He also satisfies himself that the methods of pricing, or stating, the inventory are in accordance with generally accepted accounting principles and that the practices in this respect have been adequately disclosed in the financial statements and have been observed consistently.

As a general rule, inventories are stated at the lower of cost or market. It should be borne in mind, however, that there are several different methods of determining "cost" of inventories, and the figure considered to be "market" varies with the particular circumstances. For example, the inventory *cost* may be determined by the "first-in, first-out" method, by the "last-in, first-out" method, by an averaging method, or by other acceptable methods. Similarly, *market* may, according to the circumstances, be considered to be the current replacement value of the inventory, the net amount that may reasonably be expected to be realized from the inventory in the normal course of business, or the net realizable amount reduced by an allowance for a normal profit margin.[19]

It is the CPA's duty to make sufficient tests to satisfy himself that the method, or combination of methods, used is being applied properly and consistently. To do this, it is generally necessary to make rather extensive tests of the inventory records. These tests may include comparisons of items counted with quantities shown on the records, inspection of purchase invoices, and verification of footings and extensions. They may also involve a general examination of the company's cost system, including a review of the allocation of overhead, as a check upon the pricing or valuing of inventories of work in process and finished goods.

Inventory Losses

Throughout his inventory examination the CPA is alert to see that adequate provision has been made for substantial losses on obsolete or damaged stock, discontinued products, or unsalable overruns and excess stock.

---

18 Statements on Auditing Procedure No. 12, *Amendment to Extensions of Auditing Procedure*, and No. 17, *Physical Inventories in Wartime*.

19 Accounting Research Bulletin No. 29, *Inventory Pricing*.

He satisfies himself, usually by tests of shipping and other records, that a proper cut-off has been made so that goods, the title to which has passed to the customer, are excluded from the inventory and included in sales.

Tests of purchase invoices and receiving records may be made to see that, when title for goods has passed to the company, the related liability has been recorded. The CPA also satisfies himself that adequate provision has been made for indicated losses on purchase commitments and on uncompleted sales contracts, if material.

Consigned Goods Held

Goods *held* on consignment are excluded from the inventory. To prevent substitution and to account for reported quantities, the CPA generally applies to such goods the same auditing procedures, including observation of the count, as are used on inventories to which the company has title. He often requests confirmation of the nature and quantity of the consigned goods from the consignor.

Investments

Investments may be either temporary or long-term. Temporary investments include marketable securities in which surplus funds of the company available for current operations have been invested, such as bonds and stocks of other companies and government bonds. Long-term investments include those which have been made for the purpose of control, affiliation, or other continuing business advantage. They may, or may not, be marketable.

CPA's Objectives

In auditing the investment accounts, the CPA's objectives are to assure himself that the securities recorded actually exist and are, in fact, in the possession or under the positive control of the client and that their value is stated in accordance with generally accepted accounting principles.

Accordingly, the CPA satisfies himself that securities considered to be readily convertible into cash, and in which surplus funds of the company have been invested temporarily, are shown on the balance sheet under current assets. Where stocks and bonds represent control of or a material interest in other enterprises and have a significance to the company apart from their dividend or interest return, they are more in the nature of permanent investments and he sees that they are shown below the current assets in the balance sheet. His examination is also directed to ascertaining that securities which are not readily marketable are excluded from current assets and that the basis upon which investments are shown is stated in the financial statements.

He also investigates whether the value of securities included under current assets, when priced at market quotations, amounts to materially less than the total book value so that the amount of the shrinkage should be deducted in the financial statements. In any event, if book values are shown in the balance sheet, he sees that the total amount at market quotations is stated parenthetically.

As to noncurrent investments, if examination of available data, including market quotations or, in their absence, balance sheets and income accounts supplemented by information and explanations from responsible officials, indicates that there has been a substantial shrinkage since acquisition, he sees that appropriate deductions are made or that the facts are disclosed in the financial statements. If it can be determined that the shrinkage is permanent, he satisfies himself that adequate adjustment has been made.

Procedures

As in the case of cash, the CPA's principal reliance is upon inspection and confirmation. In examining or obtaining confirmation of stocks and registered bonds, the CPA makes sure that they are in the name of the company or endorsed so as to be transferable to the company, or that they are accompanied by powers of attorney. In the case of coupon bonds, the CPA may make tests of unmatured coupons to see whether any have been cut from the bonds.

The inspection of securities is often made at the time the cash is counted. If not, the securities may be kept under control until counted. Where mortgages are held, the CPA usually requests confirmation of balances, interest status, and other pertinent information from the debtor. If mortgaged property is insurable, the CPA may review the insurance coverage. If any securities are held by depositaries or others for safekeeping or as collateral, he satisfies himself that such holder is bona fide and usually requests the holder to confirm that the securities are being held for the company. Under certain conditions confirmations are requested both at the date of the cash count and as of the balance-sheet date, if these two dates do not coincide.

The CPA's investigations of the investment accounts also provide essential information regarding investment income and profits or losses on sales of investments. As a part of these investigations, he may, therefore, prepare an analysis of security and investment income accounts for the period. In order to satisfy himself that these transactions are properly recorded, he customarily reviews evidence, such as brokers' advices, regarding purchases and sales. He may also refer to security-reporting services, or other sources, and make computations to assure himself that all dividends and interest have been entered and are correctly reported in the financial statements.

Property

Property accounts include such items as land, buildings, and machinery and equipment. In auditing these accounts, the CPA's work consists largely of a review of the principles applied, an analysis of the property accounts, and tests of the supporting data.

His review of the accounting principles applied is directed to the company's accounting practices with respect to depreciation, betterments, additions, retirements, repairs and replacements, to determine that these practices are in accordance with generally accepted accounting principles which have been consistently applied. He sees that the basis of stating the property items is adequately disclosed; including disclosure of the date of appraisal and authority for the figures when appraisal figures are used.

Property Accounts

In his analysis of the property accounts, the CPA customarily pays particular attention to the changes during the period under review. These changes consist principally of additions or betterments and sales or retirements of property items. He relies to a large extent upon inspection of supporting documents, such as authorizations by the board of directors, work orders, vouchers, journal entries, etc., in assuring himself that these changes have been properly recorded. Although the CPA takes all reasonable steps to ascertain that title to property is in the name of the company and that pledges of property through mortgage or otherwise are stated, the verification of present title and search for encumbrances are legal matters not within his province.

As a part of his analysis of the property accounts, the CPA makes sufficient tests to satisfy himself that all major items charged to them were properly capitalizable and were not proper charges to expense. In the same manner, he investigates charges to expense to satisfy himself that items which should have been capitalized were not written off. He also reviews evidence in support of recorded property sales, abandonments, or other retirements. Special inquiry may be necessary when there are no detailed records.

If the company leases its premises, the CPA generally examines the leases, noting their terms, and reviews the company's records to satisfy himself that any asset for leaseholds, as well as leasehold improvements, are being written off over their useful life or over the term of the lease, whichever is appropriate, and that significant information regarding any long-term lease arrangements is adequately disclosed.

Depreciation

The CPA's review of the company's depreciation policies is generally made in conjunction with his examination of the property accounts. In this review he satisfies himself that a reasonable allowance for depreciation has been made during the period under review and that the total amount accumulated for depreciation is adequate on the basis of a reasonable and orderly depreciation policy.[20] This does not involve or contemplate engineering studies or efforts to determine independently the useful life of the plant items. The CPA also investigates charges against accumulated depreciation and satisfies himself that they are proper. In the case of companies having diminshing assets, such as oil companies, the CPA makes a similar review and analysis of the company's policies and records concerning depletion.

When the CPA is engaged in the audit of a company for the first time, it is usually necessary to make a historical review of the property accounts in order to obtain general information relative to the acquisition of the property and the company's policies in recording it.

Intangible Assets

Intangible assets include such items as patents, trademarks, franchises, and goodwill, shown separately on the balance sheet, if practicable.[21] In auditing these accounts the CPA generally reviews the accounting records and other evidence to determine the basis used and to ascertain that the company's policies as to carrying values and amortization are in accordance with generally accepted accounting principles consistently applied. In the course of his review, he may examine pertinent documents and inquire into royalty or other agreements related to the assets.

Deferred Charges and Prepair Expenses

Deferred charges include such items as bond discount, organization expense, and other deferred items which have not been completely amortized. Such items as unexpired insurance, taxes, royalties, and other prepaid expenses are frequently included among deferred charges, although many consider it preferable to include them among current assets when they will be charged to operations within a relatively short time.[22]

With respect to these items, the CPA customarily reviews the company's practices in amortizing them and examines such evidence as insurance policies, tax receipts, contracts and invoices, making whatever computations are necessary, to determine that the amounts carried forward are applicable to future periods. In his examination of the insurance policies, he usually makes a general review of the insurance coverage, but he does not hold himself out as an expert in insurance matters.

---

20 Accounting Research Bulletin No. 33, *Depreciation and High Costs.*

21 Accounting Research Bulletin No. 24, *Accounting for Intangible Assets.*

22 Accounting Research Bulletin No. 30, *Current Assets and Current Liabilities—Working Capital.*

Other Assets

"Other Assets" may include such items as noncurrent notes and accounts receivable, deposits of various kinds, special funds, et cetera. The CPA's responsibilities for these items are the same as for current items of similar classes. When the company carries life insurance policies of which it is the beneficiary, the CPA usually satisfies himself by reference to the policies, if an approximate figure is satisfactory, that the cash surrender value is correctly stated on the financial statements; and determines by correspondence with the insurance companies whether loans have been made on the policies.

Liabilities

The audit of liabilities is designed to establish, so far as possible, that all significant liabilities are included in the financial statements, that reasonable provision has been made for accrued liabilities, and that adequate disclosure has been made of the source or type of borrowing, of any assets pledged as security for the liabilities, and of liabilities to affiliated companies and to stockholders, directors, officers, and employees, if material. In general, all liabilities to banks, trustees, and mortgagees are confirmed by correspondence. An analysis of the interest accounts often provides information regarding interest-bearing liabilities.

Notes Payable

As explained in the discussion of cash procedures, the standard form of bank confirmation ordinarily used to confirm cash balances also provides for information as to notes payable and discounted notes held by banks.

If there are any other recorded notes payable, the CPA generally obtains confirmation of the details, including the collateral held, if any, directly from the holders of the notes. The information obtained from these confirmations is compared with the accounting records to see that they are in agreement. Canceled notes are usually inspected to see that notes paid during the period have been properly discharged and to provide evidence in support of payments recorded during the period. Formal agreements made in connection with borrowings are usually reviewed to ascertain restrictions on dividends, and such covenants as those involving financial position.

Accounts Payable

The CPA customarily reconciles open items on the voucher register, or balances of the individual accounts, with the control accounts for accounts payable to see that they are in agreement. An ageing of the accounts, similar to that discussed under Accounts Receivable, may also be prepared. It is usually advisable to test whether cash discounts are taken regularly.

Large accounts which do not represent recent items, and accounts which have been active during the period but show no balance at the date of examination, are generally investigated. Confirmation of such accounts is frequently requested from the creditors by correspondence, especially when the internal control is weak. The CPA may also test whether all accounts payable are included among the liabilities by examining vouchers and payments entered in the records subsequent to the balance-sheet date, unpaid invoices not yet entered, and regular monthly statements from creditors. Receiving records both before and after the closing date may be reviewed for that purpose and to make sure that the related liabilities are recorded in the proper periods.

The CPA may also examine the records regarding goods consigned to his client to ascertain that any liabilities for the sale of such goods have been set up.

Other Current Liabilities

Accruals are usually made for other liabilities such as interest, taxes, salaries and wages, commissions, legal expenses, damages, et cetera. The CPA examines the supporting evidence, obtaining confirmation where appropriate, and makes whatever computations are necessary to be satisfied that proper accruals of the liabilities for these items have been made.

Long-Term Liabilities

Long-term liabilities include those arising from the sale of long-term notes and from mortgages and bonds. In auditing these liabilities, the CPA satisfies himself that the amount of the liability is correctly stated on the balance sheet, and that the amount of bonds in treasury or sinking funds, rates of interest, and the dates of maturity or, in the case of serial bonds, the annual or periodic maturities, are properly shown. He customarily ascertains that serial bonds, notes and mortgage installments due within a relatively short period of time, usually twelve months, are disclosed separately and, if material, are included with the current liabilities.

He also assures himself that the amount of interest expense has been properly accrued.

It is customary to request confirmation of payments on principal during the period and the amount of the debt outstanding at the balance-sheet date by direct communication with banks, trustees, or mortgagees. Bonds redeemed during or prior to the period under review are generally examined or confirmed with the trustee to ascertain that they have been properly canceled. In addition, the CPA customarily reviews loan agreements to satisfy himself that the financial requirements of the agreements are being observed and to ascertain that the significant terms of the agreements, together with any default in the principal, interest, or sinking fund provisions are disclosed and that the amounts involved are stated.

Contingent Liabilities

Businesses frequently have potential liabilities the amounts of which cannot be determined with reasonable approximation at the time of the audit.

Such liabilities might arise in connection with income taxes, notes receivable discounted, endorsements and guarantees, judgments, unfulfilled contracts, damages, et cetera. It is the CPA's duty to give due consideration to the likelihood that such contingent liabilities may become actual obligations of the company and to see that their existence is suitably noted on the financial statements if it appears that the amounts involved are or may become significant.

To satisfy himself that all significant contingent liabilities have been given recognition, the CPA customarily investigates or inquires of the most authoritative sources available for such information — including revenue agents' reports, the company's legal counsel, the banks with which the company does business, and minutes of the meetings of directors and stockholders. As in the case of actual liabilities, he usually obtains from the management of the company a representation letter enumerating all significant items of this nature.

Estimated Future Liabilities and Appropriations of Retained Income (Reserves)[23]

These items include accounts established to indicate estimates of costs or losses which it is anticipated will have to be met in the future and restrictions on the distribution of earnings. The accounts may be set up by charges against current income or by appropriations of retained income (earned surplus) depending upon the nature of the item. In auditing these accounts, the CPA generally analyzes changes during the period and investigates significant items. He satisfies himself that the accounts are properly described on the balance sheet and are used only for *the* prescribed purposes. In reviewing the accounts, the CPA pays particular attention to the company's policies in setting them up and applying them, and satisfies himself as to whether these policies are in accordance with generally accepted accounting principles.[24]

---

[23] Accounting Research Bulletin No. 34, *Recommendation of Committee on Terminology — Use of Term "Reserve."*

[24] Accounting Research Bulletin No. 28, *Accounting Treatment of General Purpose Contingency Reserves,* and No. 31, *Inventory Reserves.*

Capital Stock

Capital stock may be of different types, such as various classes of preferred and common stock. The CPA's procedures are directed to assuring himself that each of these are adequately described and properly stated in the balance sheet. This includes seeing that the capital stock or stated capital is shown on the balance sheet in accordance with the statutes of the state in which the corporation is organized, the articles of incorporation and the corporation's minutes, and that each class of stock is stated separately on the balance sheet, showing the amounts authorized, issued and outstanding and the par value per share. If the stock has no par value, the stated or assigned value per share, if any, is shown. If preferred stock, the amount of preference upon involuntary liquidation is stated, and the redemption price may also be given.

The CPA ascertains that the total amount of dividends, or the dividends per share, on outstanding cumulative preferred stock in arrears is stated and, if the arrearage creates a right to elect directors, that suitable disclosure is made. He also sees that all dividends declared but not paid at the date of the balance sheet are included in the current liabilities.

Procedures

The amounts of capital stock outstanding are usually determined by direct confirmation from the registrar and transfer agent or by reference to the stock records and stock certificate books. Changes in the amounts of stock outstanding during the period are customarily investigated by reference to cash records, or to other records of the consideration involved, and by reviewing authorizations of the board of directors and the provisions of the corporation's charter and by-laws.

The CPA also makes inquiries regarding the existence of stock options, warrants, rights, conversion privileges, or sales of stock on special terms, to satisfy himself that they have been recorded according to the facts in conformity with generally accepted accounting principles, and that the significant details of such matters are set forth in the balance sheet or in the notes thereto. If stock has been subscribed on an installment plan, it is customary to investigate whether or not payments are in arrears. If special terms have been extended to any stockholder, the minutes of the board of directors are usually examined to see that such terms have been approved.

When corporations have reacquired their own stocks, the certificates are generally examined or confirmed, and, if the company maintains its own stock records, are compared with the stock certificate books. The CPA also satisfies himself that they are adequately reported in the financial statements; preferably as a deduction from the capital stock, from surplus, or from the total of the two, at either par or cost as the laws of the state of incorporation and other relevant circumstances require. In the rare instances when temporary holdings of such stock may appropriately be treated as assets, the CPA satisfies himself that the circumstances justify such treatment and that they are indicated in the caption or in a footnote to the balance sheet. In addition, he makes sufficient investigation to assure himself that dividends on such stock are not included in income.

Other Capital Items (Capital Surplus) and Retained Income (Earned Surplus)[25]

In his examination of these accounts, the CPA generally analyzes the changes during the period and satisfies himself that they reflect the application of generally accepted accounting principles, making careful distinctions between items that should be charged to current income, to retained income, or to paid-in or other types of capital.[26] A summary of the changes in each of these accounts during the period is generally shown, either on the balance sheet or in a separate statement. The CPA also ascertains that any restrictions upon the use of these accounts are disclosed.

At the time of a "first audit," it is the CPA's responsibility to satisfy himself by appropriate investigation of the records, and by inquiries, that the balances brought forward are correctly captioned.

Income and Expense Accounts

It is generally recognized today that information as to the earnings history of a company is of vital importance both to credit grantors and to investors, and that for most purposes a statement of income is at least as important as the balance sheet. In many respects the changes in the balance sheet from year to year are more significant than the balance sheets themselves.

As stated earlier, the question of how income and expenses shall be allocated to periodic income statements is one of the basic problems of accounting and requires the exercise of experienced judgment as to the proper interpretation of all the pertinent information relating to the transactions. Because of the important part which judgment plays in these accounting decisions and in the selection and application of auditing procedures for the examination of income and expense, it is impracticable to outline specific procedures that might often be applicable to

[25] Accounting Research Bulletin No. 39, *Recommendation of Subcommittee on Terminology — Discontinuance of the Use of the Term "Surplus."*

[26] Accounting Research Bulletin No. 32, *Income and Earned Surplus,* and No. 35, *Presentation of Income and Earned Surplus.*

these accounts, such as was done with respect to the balance-sheet accounts.

General Approach

It is evident that the CPA must have a thorough understanding of the principles and classifications adopted by the company in order to use sound judgment as to the relative importance of the different items and the amount of testing needed. The extent of the testing also depends upon the effectiveness of the company's system of internal control. The tests are planned to be sufficient, when combined with information obtained in other phases of the audit, to satisfy the CPA to a reasonable extent that the transactions recorded are genuine, that they have been recorded properly, and that they have been properly classified and disclosed in the financial statements.

The CPA depends principally upon the results of careful review, tests, and analyses of the accounts with respect to items recorded during the period and upon comparison with previous periods. He usually tests the more material or extraordinary items by reference to such supporting evidence as payrolls, vouchers, journal entries, statistical data prepared by the company, copies of various kinds of agreements, budgets, and provisions of corporate minutes.

Co-ordinated with Balance-Sheet Procedures

Much of the work the CPA performs to satisfy himself as to the income and expense accounts is carried out in conjunction with his work on the balance-sheet accounts. For example, his work on sales may involve comparing sales data with the corresponding cash receipts or accounts receivable. His tests of purchases may often be co-ordinated with his tests of the cash disbursements or accounts payable records and his examination of the inventory.

Mention has been made of the necessity of assuring that proper cut-offs have been made of shipments and receipts of inventory items. Other items of income and expense, such as interest income, income from securities, interest expenses, depreciation, repairs and maintenance, taxes, amortization of deferred charges, and patents, et cetera, are likewise examined to a considerable extent in conjunction with the audit of the related asset and liability accounts.

Consolidated Statements

Consolidated financial statements present a number of auditing problems which do not arise when the audit of only one company is involved. The CPA reviews the consolidation policies followed and satisfies himself that proper recognition has been given to the business facts of the circumstances so that a fair presentation of the financial position and results of operations of the combined organizations is made.

The financial statements of subsidiaries, as well as of the parent company, are usually audited if the reporting CPA is to express an opinion on the consolidated statements. In some cases, the reporting CPA himself audits the financial statements of the subsidiaries. In other cases, the audits of some of the subsidiaries may be performed by other independent public accountants. Sometimes the accounts of relatively unimportant subsidiaries are included in the consolidation on the basis of unaudited book figures.

Consolidated Statements

So far as the audit work in connection with the consolidation of statements is concerned, the CPA's principal duty is to satisfy himself that proper adjustments have been made in combining them. These adjustments, or intercompany eliminations as they are usually called, are concerned principally with such matters as the elimination of the parent's investment accounts against the related equity accounts of the subsidiaries to be consolidated, and the elimination of intercompany transactions and intercompany profits. These are reviewed and checked to supporting data.

It is frequently desirable to audit the accounts of some of the subsidiaries as of a date prior to the close of the parent company's fiscal year. This is done so that the consolidated statements may be issued without undue delay, or so that the audit work may be spread effectively. When the subsidiaries are audited as of a prior date, it is usually necessary to review the records for the intervening period to ascertain that there have been no important transactions outside the ordinary course of business and that the financial position of the subsidiaries as of the consolidated balance-sheet date is not materially different from that at the date they were audited.

In the case of some subsidiaries, particularly foreign companies, it is frequently impossible to obtain the fiancial statements as of the date of the consolidated balance sheet in time for inclusion with the consolidated statements. It is customary to include the financial statements of such subsidiaries, if they are consolidated, as of earlier dates. The CPA is, therefore, careful to see that there have been no unusual transactions during the interim, that shipments and remittances within the consolidated group of companies up to the date of the consolidated balance sheet are taken into consideration, and that the operations of each company cover a full fiscal year. When foreign subsidiaries are included in the consolidated statements the CPA reviews the basis of conversion of foreign currencies to ascertain that it is proper and that the treatment of exchange adjustments is adequately disclosed.[27]

SUMMARY

As explained in the introduction to this pamphlet, many people hold mistaken beliefs as to the exactitude of financial statements and the responsibilities which CPAs assume in reporting upon them.

Financial statements are not completely factual. They reflect judgment as well as facts. It should not be assumed, however, that they are subject to the whims of those preparing them. Over the years, broad principles of accounting for financial transactions have been developed to guide the exercise of judgment in accounting matters. Those principles make possible the preparation of useful financial statements, but exactitude cannot be obtained.

The company has the primary responsibility for its financial statements. The CPA's function, in making an audit, is to express an opinion regarding their fairness. It is an informed, professional opinion, based on a careful examination of the accounting records and other evidence, but it is not a "certification" in the sense of being a guarantee.

In some cases, the CPA's report is brief. In others, it is quite detailed. Frequently, the CPA feels he must qualify his opinion. At times, he disclaims the expression of an opinion. It is important, therefore, to read the CPA's report carefully.

An audit is not a routine matter. Each must be designed to fit the conditions existing in the engagement. In many cases, the CPA performs part of his audit work during the year. Some audits are more extensive than others.

It should be noted that the CPA seldom reviews every transaction. On the contrary, most audits are based primarily on sampling. Experience shows that carefully planned tests of the accounting records and other data provide a high degree of assurance as to the reliability of the financial statements in most cases, but it does not insure that minor defalcations or errors will be uncovered.

In all his work, the CPA is guided by auditing standards which have been developed by the profession to assure the highest degree of professional performance. These standards relate to the personal qualifications which the CPA must possess, to his field work, and to his report. It is because of adherence to these standards that the work of CPAs has received widespread recognition.

The limitations of space inherent in a pamphlet of this kind permit

---

27 *Accounting Problems Arising from Devaluation of Foreign Currencies* — Statement by research department (American Institute of Accountants, 1949).

only a brief discussion of the principal considerations involved in making an audit. It should not be assumed that all aspects of an audit have been covered or that all procedures which might be employed in a particular case have been described. It is hoped, however, that the pamphlet has established a better understanding of the nature of financial statements and that it has provided a clearer view of how the CPA makes an audit and the responsibilities he assumes in expressing an opinion on financial statements.

Index

Accounting Books Published by Garland

NEW BOOKS

■ *Altman, Edward I., *The Prediction of Corporate Bankruptcy: A Discriminant Analysis.*
New York, 1988.

■ Ashton, Robert H., ed. *The Evolution of Accounting Behavior Research: An Overview.*
New York, 1984.

■ Ashton, Robert H., ed. *Some Early Contributions to the Study of Audit Judgement.*
New York, 1984.

■ *Bodenhorn, Diran. *Economic Accounting.*
New York, 1988.

---

* Included in the Garland series Foundations of Accounting
† Included in the Academy of Accounting Historians, Classics Series, Gary John Previt, ed.

■ *Bougen, Philip D. *Accounting and Industrial Relations: Some Historical Evidence on Their Interaction.*
New York, 1988.

■ Brief, Richard P., ed. *Corporate Financial Reporting and Analysis in the Early 1900s.*
New York, 1986.

■ Brief, Richard P., ed. *Depreciation and Capital Maintenance.*
New York, 1984.

■ Brief, Richard P., ed. *Estimating the Economic Rate of Return from Accounting Data.*
New York, 1986.

■ Brief, Richard P., ed. *Four Classics on the Theory of Double-Entry Bookkeeping.*
New York, 1982.

■ Chambers, R. J., and G. W. Dean, eds. *Chambers on Accounting.*
New York, 1986.
Volume I: Accounting, Management and Finance.
Volume II: Accounting Practice and Education.
Volume III: Accounting Theory and Research.
Volume IV: Price Variation Accounting.
Volume V: Continuously Contemporary Accounting.

■ *Clark, John B. (with a new introduction by Donald Dewey). *Capital and Its Earnings.*
New York, 1988.

■ Clarke, F. L. *The Tangled Web of Price Variation Accounting: The Development of Ideas Underlying Professional Prescriptions in Six Countries.*
New York, 1982.

■ Coopers & Lybrand. *The Early History of Coopers & Lybrand.*
New York, 1984.

■ Craswell, Allen. *Audit Qualifications in Australia 1950 to 1979.*
New York, 1986.

■ Dean, G. W., and M. C. Wells, eds. *The Case for Continuously Contemporary Accounting.*
New York, 1984.

■ Dean, G. W. , and M. C. Wells, eds. *Forerunners of Realizable Values Accounting in Financial Reporting.*
New York, 1982.

■ Edey, Harold C. *Accounting Queries.*
New York, 1982.

■ Edwards, J. R., ed. *Legal Regulation of British Company Accounts 1836-1900.*
New York, 1986.

■ Edwards, J. R. ed. *Reporting Fixed Assets in Nineteenth-Century Company Accounts.*
New York, 1986.

■ Edwards, J. R., ed. *Studies of Company Records: 1830-1974.*
New York, 1984.

■ Fabricant, Solomon. *Studies in Social and Private Accounting.*
New York, 1982.

■ Gaffikin, Michael, and Michael Aitkin, eds. *The Development of Accounting Theory: Significant Contributors to Accounting Thought in the 20th Century.*
New York, 1982.

■ Hawawini, Gabriel A., ed. *Bond Duration and Immunization: Early Developments and Recent Contributions.*
New York, 1982.

■ Hawawini, Gabriel A., and Pierre A. Michel, eds. *European Equity Markets: Risk, Return, and Efficiency.*
New York, 1984.

■ Hawawini, Gabriel A., and Pierre Michel. *Mandatory Financial Information and Capital Market Equilibrium in Belgium.*
New York, 1986.

■ Hawkins, David F. *Corporate Financial Disclosure, 1900-1933: A Study of Management Inertia within a Rapidly Changing Environment.*
New York, 1986.

■ *Hopwood, Anthony G. *Accounting from the Outside: The Collected Papers of Anthony G. Hopwood.*
New York, 1988.

■ Johnson, H. Thomas. *A New Approach to Management Accounting History.*
New York, 1986.

■ Kinney, William R., ed. *Fifty Years of Statistical Auditing.*
New York, 1986.

■ Klemstine, Charles E., and Michael W. Maher. *Management Accounting Research: A Review and Annotated Bibliography.*
New York, 1984.

■ *Langenderfer, Harold Q., and Grover L. Porter, eds. *Rational Accounting Concepts: The Writings of Willard Graham.*
New York, 1988.

■ *Lee, T. A., ed. *The Evolution of Audit Thought and Practice.*
New York, 1988.

■ Lee, T. A., ed. *A Scottish Contribution to Accounting History.*
New York, 1986.

■ Lee, T. A. *Towards a Theory and Practice of Cash Flow Accounting.*
New York, 1986.

■ Lee, T. A., ed. *Transactions of the Chartered Accountants Students' Societies of Edinburgh and Glasgow: A Selection of Writings, 1886-1958.*
New York, 1984.

■ *Loft, Anne. *Understanding Accounting in Its Social and Historical Context: The Case of Cost Accounting in Britain, 1914-1925.*
New York, 1988.

■ McKinnon, Jill L.. *The Historical Development and Operational Form of Corporate Reporting Regulation in Japan.*
New York, 1986.

■ *McMickle, Peter L., and Paul H. Jensen, eds. *The Auditor's Guide of 1869: A Review and Computer Enhancement of Recently Discovered Old Microfilm of America's First Book on Auditing by H. J. Mettenheimer.*
New York, 1988.

■ *McMickle, Peter L., and Paul H. Jensen, eds. *The Birth of American Accountancy: A Bibliographic Analysis of Works on Accounting Published in America through 1820.*
New York, 1988.

■ *Mepham, M.-J. *Accounting in Eighteenth-Century Scotland.*
New York, 1988.

■ *Mills, Patti A., trans. *The Legal Literature of Accounting: On Accounts by Diego del Castillo.*
New York, 1988.

■ *Murphy, George J. *The Evolution of Canadian Corporate Reporting Practices: 1900-1970.*
New York, 1988.

■ *Mumford, Michael J., ed. *Edward Stamp—Later Papers.*
New York, 1988.

■ Nobes, Christopher, ed. *The Development of Double Entry: Selected Essays.*
New York, 1984.

- Nobes, Christopher. *Issues in International Accounting.*
  New York, 1986.

- Parker, Lee D. *Developing Control Concepts in the 20th Century.*
  New York, 1986.

- *Parker, Lee D., ed. *Financial Reporting to Employees: From Past to Present.*
  New York, 1988.

- *Parker, Lee D., and O. Finley Graves, eds. *Methodology and Method in History: A Bibliography.*
  New York, 1988.

- Parker, R. H. *Papers on Accounting History.*
  New York, 1984.

- Previts, Gary John, and Alfred R. Roberts, eds. *Federal Securities Law and Accounting 1933-1970: Selected Addresses.*
  New York, 1986.

- *Reid, Jean Margo, ed. *Law and Accounting: Nineteenth-Century American Legal Cases.*
  New York, 1988.

- *Sheldahl, Terry K., ed. *Accounting Literature in the United States before Mitchell and Jones (1796): Contributions by Four English Writers, through American Editions, and Two Pioneer Local Authors.*
  New York, 1988.

■ Sheldahl, Terry K. *Beta Alpha Psi, from Alpha to Omega: Pursuing a Vision of Professional Education for Accountants, 1919-1945.*
New York, 1982.

■ Sheldahl, Terry K. *Beta Alpha Psi, from Omega to Zeta Omega: The Making of a Comprehensive Accounting Fraternity, 1946-1984.*
New York, 1986.

■ *Sheldahl, Terry K., ed. *Education for the Mercantile Countinghouse: Critical and Constructive Essays by Nine British Writers, 1716-1794.*
New York, 1988.

■ Solomons, David. *Collected Papers on Accounting and Accounting Education (in two volumes).*
New York, 1984.

■ Sprague, Charles F. *The General Principles of the Science of Accounts and the Accountancy of Investment.*
New York, 1984.

■ Stamp, Edward. *Edward Stamp—Later Papers. See* Michael J. Mumford.

■ Stamp, Edward. *Selected Papers on Accounting, Auditing, and Professional Problems.*
New York, 1984.

■ *Staubus, George J. *Activity Costing for Decisions: Cost Accounting in the Decision Usefulness Framework.*
New York, 1988.

■ Storrar, Colin, ed. *The Accountant's Magazine—An Anthology.*
New York, 1986.

■ Tantral, Panadda. *Accounting Literature in Non-Accounting Journals: An Annotated Bibliography.*
New York, 1984.

■ *Vangermeersch, Richard G. *Alexander Hamilton Church: A Man of Ideas for All Seasons.*
New York, 1988.

■ Vangermeersch, Richard, ed. *The Contributions of Alexander Hamilton Church to Accounting and Management.*
New York, 1986.

■ Vangermeersch, Richard, ed. *Financial Accounting Milestones in the Annual Reports of the United States Steel Corporation—The First Seven Decades.*
New York, 1986.

■ *Walker, Stephen P. *The Society of Accountants in Edinburgh, 1854-1914: A Study of Recruitment to a New Profession.*
New York, 1988.

■ Whitmore, John. *Factory Accounts.*
New York, 1984.

■ *Whittred, Greg. *The Evolution of Consolidated Financial Reporting in Australia: An Evaluation of an Alternative Hypothesis.*
New York, 1988.

■ Yamey, Basil S. *Further Essays on the History of Accounting.*
New York, 1982.

■ Zeff, Stephen A., ed. *The Accounting Postulates and Principles Controversy of the 1960s.*
New York, 1982.

■ Zeff, Stephen A., ed. *Accounting Principles Through the Years: The Views of Professional and Academic Leaders 1938-1954.*
New York, 1982.

■ Zeff, Stephen A., and Maurice Moonitz, eds. *Sourcebook on Accounting Principles and Auditing Procedures: 1917-1953 (in two volumes).*
New York, 1984.

■ *Zeff, Stephen a., ed. *The U. S. Accounting Profession in the 1890s and Early 1900s.*
New York, 1988.

REPRINTED TITLES

■ *American Institute of Accountants. *Accountants Index, 1920* (in two volumes).
New York, 1921 (Garland reprint, 1988).

■ American Institute of Accountants. *Fiftieth Anniversary Celebration.*
Chicago, 1937 (Garland reprint, 1982).

■ American Institute of Accountants. *Library Catalogue.*
New York, 1919 (Garland reprint, 1982).

■ Arthur Andersen Company. *The First Fifty Years 1913-1963.*
Chicago, 1963 (Garland reprint, 1984).

■ Bevis, Herman W. *Corporate Financial Reporting in a Competitive Economy.*
New York, 1965 (Garland reprint, 1986).

■ Bonini,. Charles P., Robert K. Jaedicke, and Harvey M. Wagner, eds. *Management Controls: New Directions in Basic Research.*
New York, 1964 (Garland reprint, 1986).

■ **The Book-Keeper and the American Counting Room.*
New York, 1880-1884 (Garland reprint, 1988).

▪ Bray, F. Sewell. *Four Essays in Accounting Theory.* London, 1953. *Bound with* Institute of Chartered Accountants in England and Wales and the National Institute of Economic and Social Research. *Some Accounting Terms and Concepts.*
Cambridge, 1951 (Garland reprint, 1982).

▪ Brown, R. Gene, and Kenneth S. Johnston. *Paciolo on Accounting.*
New York, 1963 (Garland reprint, 1984).

▪ Carey, John L., and William O. Doherty, eds. *Ethical Standards of the Accounting Profession.*
New York, 1966 (Garland reprint, 1986).

▪ Chambers, R. J. *Accounting in Disarray.*
Melbourne, 1973 (Garland reprint, 1982).

▪ Cooper, Ernest. *Fifty-seven years in an Accountant's Office.* *See* Sir Russell Kettle.

▪ Couchman, Charles B. *The Balance-Sheet.*
New York, 1924 (Garland reprint, 1982).

▪ Couper, Charles Tennant. *Report of the Trial ... Against the Directors and Manager of the City of Glasgow Bank.*
Edinburgh, 1879 (Garland reprint, 1984).

▪ Cutforth, Arthur E. *Audits.*
London, 1906 (Garland reprint, 1982).

▪ Cutforth, Arthur E. *Methods of Amalgamation.*
London, 1926 (Garland reprint, 1982).

■ Deinzer, Harvey T. *Development of Accounting Thought.*
New York, 1965 (Garland reprint, 1984).

■ De Paula, F.R.M. *The Principles of Auditing.*
London, 1915 (Garland reprint, 1984).

■ Dickerson, R. W. *Accountants and the Law of Negligence.*
Toronto, 1966 (Garland reprint, 1982).

■ Dodson, James. *The Accountant, or, the Method of Bookkeeping Deduced from Clear Principles, and Illustrated by a Variety of Examples.*
London, 1750 (Garland reprint, 1984).

■ Dyer, S. *A Common Sense Method of Double Entry Bookkeeping, on First Principles, as Suggested by De Morgan. Part I, Theoretical.*
London, 1897 (Garland reprint, 1984).

■ *† Edwards, James Don. *History of Public Accounting in the United States.*
East Lansing, 1960 (Garland reprint, 1988).

■ *† Edwards, James Don, and Robert F. Salmonson. *Contributions of Four Accounting Pioneers: Kohler, Littleton, May, Paton.*
East Lancing, 1961 (Garland reprint, 1988).

■ *The Fifth International Congress on Accounting, 1938 [Kongress-Archiv 1938 des V. Internationalen Prüfungs- und Treuhand-Kongresses].*
Berlin, 1938 (Garland reprint, 1986).

■ Finney, A. H. *Consolidated Statements.*
New York, 1922 (Garland reprint, 1982).

■ Fisher, Irving. *The Rate of Interest.*
New York, 1907 (Garland reprint, 1982).

■ Florence, P. Sargant. *Economics of Fatigue and Unrest and the Efficiency of Labour in English and American Industry.*
London, 1923 (Garland reprint, 1984).

■ *Fourth International Congress on Accounting 1933.*
London, 1933 (Garland reprint, 1982).

■ Foye, Arthur B. *Haskins & Sells: Our First Seventy-Five Years.*
New York, 1970 (Garland reprint, 1984).

■ *† Garner, Paul S. *Evolution of Cost Accounting to 1925.*
University, Alabama, 1925 (Garland reprint, 1988).

■ Garnsey, Sir Gilbert. *Holding Companies and Their Published Accounts.* London, 1923. *Bound with* Sir Gilbert Garnsey. *Limitations of a Balance Sheet.*
London, 1928 (Garland reprint, 1982).

■ Garrett, A. A. *The History of the Society of Incorporated Accountants, 1885-1957.*
Oxford, 1961 (Garland reprint, 1984).

■ Gilman, Stephen. *Accounting Concepts of Profit.*
New York, 1939 (Garland reprint, 1982).

■ Gordon, William. *The Universal Accountant, and Complete Merchant* ... [Volume II].
Edinburgh, 1765 (Garland reprint, 1986).

■ Green, Wilmer. *History and Survey of Accountancy.*
Brooklyn, 1930 (Garland reprint, 1986).

■ Hamilton, Robert. *An Introduction to Merchandise, Parts IV and V (Italian Bookkeeping and Practical Bookkeeping).*
Edinburgh, 1788 (Garland reprint, 1982).

■ Hatton, Edward. *The Merchant's Magazine; or, Tradesman's Treasury.* London, 1695 (Garland reprint, 1982).
Hills, George S. *The Law of Accounting and Financial Statements.*
Boston, 1957 (Garland reprint, 1982).

■ *A History of Cooper Brothers & Co. 1854 to 1954.*
London, 1954 (Garland reprint, 1986).

■ Hofstede, Geert. *The Game of Budget Control.*
Assen, 1967 (Garland reprint, 1984).

■ Howitt, Sir Harold. *The History of the Institute of Chartered Accountants in England and Wales 1880-1965, and of Its Founder Accountancy Bodies 1870-1880.*
London, 1966 (Garland reprint, 1984).

■ Institute of Chartered Accountants in England and Wales and The National Institute of Social and Economic Research. *Some Accounting Terms and Concepts. See* F. Sewell Bray.

■ Institute of Chartered Accountants of Scotland. *History of the Chartered Accountants of Scotland from the Earliest Times to 1954.*
Edinburgh, 1954 (Garland reprint, 1984).

■ *International Congress on Accounting 1929.*
New York, 1930 (Garland reprint, 1982).

■ Jaedicke, Robert K., Yuji Ijiri, and Oswald Nielsen, eds. *Research in Accounting Measurement.*
American Accounting Association,
1966 (Garland reprint, 1986).

■ Keats, Charles. *Magnificent Masquerade.*
New York, 1964 (Garland reprint, 1982).

■ Kettle, Sir Russell. *Deloitte & Co. 1854-1956.* Oxford, 1958. *Bound with* Ernest Cooper. *Fifty-seven Years in an Accountant's Office.*
London, 1921 (Garland reprint, 1982).

■ Kitchen, J., and R. H. Parker. *Accounting Thought and Education: Six English Pioneers.*
London, 1980 (Garland reprint, 1984).

■ Lacey, Kenneth. *Profit Measurement and Price Changes.*
London, 1952 (Garland reprint, 1982).

■ Lee, Chauncey. *The American Accomptant.*
Lansingburgh, 1797 (Garland reprint, 1982).

■ Lee, T. A., and R. H. Parker. *The Evolution of Corporate Financial Reporting.*
Middlesex, 1979 (Garland reprint, 1984).

■ *† Littleton, A. C.. *Accounting Evolution to 1900.*
New York, 1933 (Garland reprint, 1988).

■ Malcolm, Alexander. *The Treatise of Book-Keeping, or, Merchants Accounts; In the Italian Method of Debtor and Creditor; Wherein the Fundamental Principles of That Curious and Approved Method Are Clearly and Fully Explained and Demonstrated ... To Which Are Added, Instructions for Gentlemen of Land Estates, and Their Stewards or Factors: With Directions Also for Retailers, and Other More Private Persons.*
London, 1731 (Garland reprint, 1986).

■ Meij, J. L., ed. *Depreciation and Replacement Policy.*
Chicago, 1961 (Garland reprint, 1986).

■ Newlove, George Hills. *Consolidated Balance Sheets.*
New York, 1926 (Garland reprint, 1982).

■ North, Roger. *The Gentleman Accomptant; or, An Essay to Unfold the Mystery of Accompts; By Way of Debtor and Creditor, Commonly Called Merchants Accompts, and Applying the Same to the Concerns of the Nobility and Gentry of England.*
London 1714 (Garland reprint, 1986).

■ **Proceedings of the Seventh International Congress of Accountants.* Amsterdam, 1957 (Garland reprint, 1988).

■ Pryce-Jones, Janet E., and R. H. Parker. *Accounting in Scotland: A Historical Bibliography.*
Edinburgh, 1976 (Garland reprint, 1984).

■ *Reynolds, W. B., and F. W. Thornton. *Duties of a Junior Accountant* [three editions].
New York, 1917, 1933, 1953
(Garland reprint, 1988).

■ Robinson, H. W. *A History of Accountants in Ireland.*
Dublin, 1964 (Garland edition, 1984).

■ Robson, T. B. *Consolidated and Other Group Accounts.*
London, 1950 (Garland reprint, 1982).

■ Rorem, C. Rufus. *Accounting Method.*
Chicago, 1928 (Garland reprint, 1982).

■ Saliers, Earl A., ed. *Accountants' Handbook.*
New York, 1923 (Garland reprint, 1986).

■ Samuel, Horace B. *Shareholder's Money.*
London, 1933 (Garland reprint, 1982).

■ *The Securitites and Exchange Commission in the Matter of McKesson & Robbins, Inc. Report on Investigation.*
Washington, D. C., 1940 (Garland reprint, 1982).

■ *The Securities and Exchange Commission in the Matter of McKesson & Robbins, Inc. Testimony of Expert Witnesses.*
Washington, D. C., 1939 (Garland reprint, 1982).

■ Shaplen, Roger. *Kreuger: Genius and Swindler.*
New York, 1960 (Garland reprint, 1986).

■ Singer, H. W. *Standardized Accountancy in Germany. (With a new appendix.)*
Cambridge, 1943 (Garland reprint, 1982).

■ *The Sixth International Congress on Accounting.*
London, 1952 (Garland reprint, 1984).

■ Stewart, Jas. C. (with a new introductory note by T. A. Lee). *Pioneers of a Profession: Chartered Accountants to 1879.*
Edinburgh, 1977 (Garland reprint, 1986).

■ Thompson, Wardbaugh. *The Accomptant's Oracle: or, a Key to Science, Being a Compleat Practical System of Book-keeping.*
York, 1777 (Garland reprint, 1984).

■ *Thornton, F. W. *Duties of the Senior Accountant.* New York, 1932. *Bound with.* John C. Martin. *Duties of Junior and Senior Accountants, Supplement of the CPA Handbook.*
New York, 1953 (Garland reprint, 1988).

■ Vatter, William J. *Managerial Accounting.*
New York, 1950 (Garland reprint, 1986).

■ Woolf, Arthur H. *A Short History of Accountants and Accountancy.*
London, 1912 (Garland reprint, 1986).

■ Yamey, B. S., H. C. Edey, and Hugh W. Thomson. *Accounting in England and Scotland: 1543-1800.*
London, 1963 (Garland reprint, 1982).